W9-ASY-558

# WELFARE
# REFORM

A Reference Handbook

Other Titles in ABC-CLIO's
# CONTEMPORARY
# WORLD ISSUES
Series

Books in the Contemporary World Issues series address vital issues in today's society such as terrorism, sexual harassment, homelessness, AIDS, gambling, animal rights, and air pollution. Written by professional writers, scholars, and nonacademic experts, these books are authoritative, clearly written, up-to-date, and objective. They provide a good starting point for research by high school and college students, scholars, and general readers, as well as by legislators, businesspeople, activists, and others.

Each book, carefully organized and easy to use, contains an overview of the subject; a detailed chronology; biographical sketches; facts and data and/or documents and other primary-source material; a directory of organizations and agencies; annotated lists of print and nonprint resources; a glossary; and an index.

Readers of books in the Contemporary World Issues series will find the information they need in order to better understand the social, political, environmental, and economic issues facing the world today.

# WELFARE
# REFORM

## A Reference Handbook

### Mary Ellen Hombs

## CONTEMPORARY
## WORLD ISSUES

### ABC-CLIO

Santa Barbara, California
Denver, Colorado
Oxford, England

**Library of Congress Cataloging-in-Publication Data**

Hombs, Mary Ellen.
  Welfare reform : a reference handbook / Mary Ellen Hombs.
    p. cm.—(Contemporary world issues)
  Includes bibliographical references and index.
  ISBN 0-87436-844-8 (alk. paper)
    1. Public welfare—United States—Handbooks, manuals, etc.
  I. Title. II. Series.
  HV95.H554   1996
  361.973—dc21                                                            96-47515

02 01 00 99 98 97       10 9 8 7 6 5 4 3 2

ABC-CLIO, Inc.
130 Cremona Drive, P.O. Box 1911
Santa Barbara, California 93116-1911

This book is printed on acid-free paper ∞ .
Manufactured in the United States of America

# Contents

# Preface

Welfare reform has been a key political theme in national policy debate during the 1990s. It has made the headlines day after day as politicians and legislators have argued about the costs of social welfare programs, the characteristics of the people who use the programs, and the effectiveness of various efforts to assist poor and working people. Competing philosophies have been offered to the American people in this debate, which has frequently occurred at both high speed and high volume. The public debate has had many purposes, and it has been complex and lengthy. It has taken place in the U.S. Congress, in statehouses across the country, and in a variety of other settings.

Most policy debates that engender such strong feeling and widespread response are complicated at their roots, relying sometimes on questions such as public spending or fiscal responsibility. At other times, they rely on issues that may have a moral, emotional, or personal basis for many people. For example, what do we owe to others who do not have adequate food, shelter, or income? While legislative reform of the federal cash assistance programs remains unresolved after several years of debate, virtually everyone has an opinion on the debate and the desired outcome.

The purpose of this book is to examine the welfare reform debate about proposed major changes in existing federal and state programs to assist poor people. It will also help the reader understand some of the issues and questions behind the debate and some of the overarching political themes that tie the "welfare reform" discussion to other larger political developments. This book is not a history of welfare programs in this country, although it briefly examines the historical roots of existing programs. It does not offer a philosophical defense of any of the theories of how best to assist people in poverty, although it does identify what are often competing or conflicting ideas about this goal. It also tries to distinguish the rhetoric of the debate from issues or research in other arenas. To do so, it tries to untangle the public debate and rhetoric about programs, their beneficiaries, and their results from the facts. It is not a book about poverty itself, although of necessity it examines some aspects of poverty that have been central to current reform efforts.

This book provides reference material to explain some of the key issues in the debate, distinguish some of the often complicated themes that are part of it, and lead to useful resources for further information. Chapter 1 is a general look at some of the current public policy discussion and its roots. Its goal is to segregate some of the competing purposes that have led to often raucous policy discussion. Chapter 2 provides a chronology of key events in the history of the nation's social welfare programs, as well as important developments during the current debate.

The welfare reform debate centers on the nation's primary cash assistance program, which serves poor single mothers. The most identifiable critical participants in this debate, however, are not the beneficiaries of the programs but policymakers, legislators, and academics. Brief descriptions of some of these individuals make up Chapter 3.

Any vital public debate is marked by the trading of arguments and counterarguments. Each side claims to have the facts and accuses the other of spreading myths. Chapter 4 offers some background information on social welfare programs, beneficiaries of those programs, and public opinion about the programs and recipients of benefits. Chapter 5 contains excerpts from documents related to the debate. Chapter 6 offers analysis of the key themes in legislation put forth in the two houses of the U.S. Congress. A new law passed in 1996 will bring major changes. A summary of issues covered in litigation around social welfare programs is also included.

As is true in many contemporary debates, much of the important writing and analysis takes places outside the traditional channels of information for researchers and readers. Some is published by issue-oriented organizations, some by government agencies, and some by academics. To aid the reader in finding some of these current materials, Chapter 7 offers a listing of some organizations and agencies, Chapter 8 provides a bibliography of print resources on welfare reform issues, and Chapter 9 lists non-print resources.

Welfare reform and social welfare programs have their own unique vocabulary, which includes budget and legislative terms, as well as a wealth of acronyms. Some of the key terms are defined in the glossary.

Whatever the outcome of the welfare reform debate, the critical questions raised will remain part of the ongoing discussion in this country. The 1990s are not the first time these issues have come to the forefront of policy discussion, nor are the proposed remedies new except in their timing. While this new law will make drastic changes in existing programs, it is important to remember that the social welfare programs themselves were not always a part of the federal government, or even an accepted federal or state duty.

# Overview 1

In the early 1990s, increasing public concern about growing numbers of welfare recipients, long-term dependence on welfare programs (primarily the Aid to Families with Dependent Children [AFDC] program), and the rate of children being born outside marriage focused public attention on the nation's social welfare system. There was increased concern about the number of teenage mothers in the nation. Proposals to change these programs, including their rules and use, are popularly referred to as "welfare reform."

Public policy debate about federal welfare reform began during the 1992 presidential campaign and escalated after that. The debate was a centerpiece of the work of the 104th Congress, which began its work in January 1995 after a Republican sweep of the off-year elections. New Republican members elected under a collective public agreement called the Contract with America made welfare reform part of a ten-point pledge to the American public. More than 20 bills were introduced in Congress to change the welfare system. Titles of just two prominent bills demonstrate the themes at work in the debate as a whole: the Work and Responsibility Act and the Personal Responsibility Act.

While President Bill Clinton started the focus on welfare reform by pledging as a presidential candidate in 1992 to "end welfare as we know it," the debate was scarcely new. But with the 104th Congress, the debate escalated and the reform proposals multiplied. After repeated efforts to pass legislation that President Clinton would sign (he vetoed earlier legislation), the Personal Responsibility and Work Opportunity Reconciliation Act of 1996 (H.R. 3734) was passed by both houses of Congress in August 1996. It was signed by President Clinton on 22 August 1996. The new law ends decades of federal protection for the guarantee of cash assistance to the poor.

As with the health care reform debate of the early 1990s, each side in the debate promised significant positive change from its proposals and forecast national doom and suffering if either the status quo was untouched or the opposing plan passed. Many new Republican members portrayed themselves as agents of change. They characterized long-term Democratic members as people whose ideas and social welfare programs had failed and should no longer be defended. In turn, Democratic members promised that children would be the victims of Republican reform proposals.

# A Brief History of Welfare Programs

The modern era of welfare programs in the United States can be traced to the years of the Great Depression following the stock market crash of 1929. Millions of people were thrown into unemployment as a result of the impact on the economy. Banks and factories closed. Soup kitchens opened. People left their homes to look for work elsewhere in the country. When Franklin Delano Roosevelt took office as president in 1933, many people were in dire need. Roosevelt brought to the presidency his experiences as governor of New York, where he had overhauled the public welfare law, instituted old-age pensions, and developed other social programs. As a result of Roosevelt's New Deal policies, there were four primary developments in the nation's welfare system: social security, Aid to Dependent Children (ADC), workmen's compensation, and unemployment insurance.

The welfare reform debate of the 1990s has centered on the AFDC program (which succeeded ADC when it was decided later to include the needs of the custodial parent in the calculation of benefits). But it was the Social Security program that was the controversial element of the Roosevelt initiatives at that time. It was criticized as too conservative a measure and was also viewed as a drastic step toward socialism. This is important to note because it underscores the reality that what is politically controversial in one era may not attract much attention in another.

The passage of the Social Security Act established federal responsibility for public welfare. This was an important development in a nation whose history had been based on the Poor Laws of colonial times. The idea of local responsibility for the needy was deeply rooted in Western Europe. Federal responsibility was further defined in 1953 when the Department of Health, Education, and Welfare was established as the cabinet agency responsible for federal initiatives dealing with welfare, social security, and related issues.

The purposes of the Roosevelt programs should also be noted. They were intended to help people who had experienced bad luck, suffered a misfortune, or could somehow be viewed as blameless for their predicament. These are the "deserving" poor, those who want to work but can't, those who don't wish to receive charity or a handout, but must do so to keep home and family together. In fact, ensuring that a child could be raised in the home was the original purpose of AFDC.

Social security and workmen's compensation were to aid those from whom work could not or should not be expected because of age or infirmity. The AFDC program was established as a program with both federal and state financial participation. It built on the existing tradition of state pensions for widows who were mothers of small children. In 1934, 45 states had widows' pension laws in place. Although it stands in contrast to current trends, it was then viewed as undesirable for these women to have to go to work to support their children, when it would mean the absence of the mother from the home and children left to fend for themselves. Better to provide a small income so the mother could maintain her family. Otherwise the income programs did not aim to help people simply because of their poverty but because of age or infirmity. Further, by focusing their relief on those who could be held blameless for their circumstances, AFDC sought to uphold the tradition of distinguishing between those "undeserving" poor whose aim was possibly to exploit the community's resources and those who truly needed assistance (Trattner 1974).

Concepts about destitution, dignity, self-sufficiency, and work have very deep roots in the nation and in the practices carried out by public programs in any given era. While the programs of the 1930s produced an official acknowledgment that hard times might be caused by economic and social forces larger than the individual, it was not the goal to offer long-term help or assistance that produced a living standard higher than work would offer. Work was the goal and expectation for men. The AFDC program sought to keep poor mothers in the home, which was in keeping with the times. The debate about welfare reform in the 1990s reflects the times as well: it seeks to provide assistance, but with the expectation that a person will work if at all possible, regardless of gender. It also builds on the 1988 reform effort of the Family Support Act, which shifted emphasis to employment.

In his inaugural address in 1961, President John F. Kennedy stated that "the hand of hope must be extended to the poor and oppressed." The 1960s brought a greater awareness of poverty and inequality in the United States and around the world. By 1963, when clergymember and civil rights leader Rev. Martin Luther King, Jr., led over 200,000 people in a march at the Lincoln Memorial, this awareness was at a high point. King's "I Have a Dream" speech marked a historic event in the civil rights movement of the 1960s, which drew the nation's attention to these issues. In 1964, with Democratic President Lyndon B. Johnson succeeding Kennedy, there was a new call to Congress to enact a 13-point program to declare "unconditional war on poverty" in the United States. The Economic Opportunity Act passed later that year created VISTA, the Job Corps, Head Start, community action programs, and other programs. These were the programs of the "Great Society" and the hallmark of the liberal Democratic philosophy that government can and should act to help people. In 1965 Johnson signed into law the Social Security Act amendments that created the Medicare and Medicaid programs. The urban riots of the 1960s continued to focus attention on poverty. In 1968 the Kerner Commission, reporting on its investigation of major civil rights riots in urban areas in 1967, announced that earlier civil rights gains had done little to improve the quality of life for poor urban black people.

In 1969 Republican President Richard Nixon called for drastic change in the nation's welfare system, proposing the Family Assistance Plan, which would alter programs unchanged since the 1930s. The Nixon plan proposed that every unemployed family of four would receive at least $1,600 a year from the federal government. This assistance was designed to provide the difference between low wages and what was needed to live above the poverty line. Working poor people would be allowed to keep more of their pay under the plan, and all able-bodied people (except mothers with small children) would be required to work or be in a job-training program. The idea that mothers would no longer be paid to stay at home with their children represented a huge shift in emphasizing work over all else and was highly controversial. In a plan called the "new federalism" the program would eventually be turned over to the states. The proposal provoked immediate debate and ultimately failed in Congress.

Nevertheless, Congress continued to create new programs. In 1972, it passed the Supplemental Security Income program to provide a cash income to poor elderly and disabled adults unable to work. Needy children were also included to help their families with extra expenses resulting from a child's disabilities. In the two decades since then, important changes have occurred through congressional action and the initiatives of the states.

## Recent History

The recent history of the AFDC program has shaped the welfare reform debate of the 1990s. One event occurred at the federal level, via legislation. The other is a federal initiative to give greater latitude to the states to implement their own reform efforts. Due to the slow pace of federal legislation on welfare reform, the freedom given to the states to undertake their own experimental programs has caused broad change at the state level of welfare programs.

The first key development was the passage in 1988 of the last previous piece of major welfare reform legislation, the Family Support Act (FSA). The FSA underscored the relation to work that has been so important in the debate of the 1990s. This law required the states to establish statewide Job Opportunities and Basic Skills Training Programs (JOBS) by 1992. JOBS expanded the number of families who were required to be in work programs, and it required states to provide a range of education, training, and job-readiness programs. States were also required to provide transportation, supportive services, and child care for participants. The FSA also demonstrated the continuing federal role in directing the action of the states, but it set a new standard in permitting state choice in implementation.

The second important event behind the growing welfare reform debate was the action of the Bush administration in early 1992 when changes were set in motion around what are called waivers. Waivers are state actions to seek the waiving of federal rules for the AFDC program, so that a state can carry out an experimental, pilot, or demonstration program that would otherwise not be consistent with federal requirements. Bush changed the federal waiver process to make the federal government more receptive to waiver requests by the states and prepared to act on them speedily. In his 1992 State of the Union message, he urged states to "replace the assumptions of the welfare state and help reform the welfare system" (*New York Times* 1992).

Two key requirements govern the granting of waivers. First, the state's proposal must be "cost-neutral" to the federal government. Second, whatever project the state undertakes (eliminating restrictions on eligibility of two-parent families, for instance) must be carefully evaluated by the state. No waiver requests were rejected by the Bush administration after this new policy. Forty-two states submitted waiver requests after the 1992 announcement, and 37 states had waiver projects in effect in mid-1996.

Although welfare reform legislation at the federal level frequently was in stalemate during the Clinton administration, many governors were ready to change their welfare programs for economic, social, or political reasons. One way to effect this change while waiting for the U.S. Congress to act was to seek a waiver. In fact, actions taken by the Reagan administration in the early 1980s were the successors to state actions of the previous decade, and when presidential candidate and Arkansas Gov. Bill Clinton promised to "end welfare as we know it," he was putting his credentials with Arkansas' waiver programs into the debate. The Clinton administration continued and expanded the policy of speedy and favorable review (Greenberg 1996).

An examination of the waivers sought by states reveals certain areas of overlap in waiver requests. Together they stress work, family, and personal responsibility, the themes of the 1990s debate. At least 20 states sought waivers in the following program areas:

- removing restrictions so that two-parent families are eligible to receive AFDC;

- family caps that restrict the size of the grant a family receives when an additional child is born to a mother already on AFDC;

- child care changes that extend or expand the availability of child care assistance for AFDC recipients;

- increased disregard of earnings, which assists people who go to work to keep a greater portion of their earnings;

- greater penalties for violating AFDC rules for those not in compliance with JOBS requirements;

- increased program asset limits (the $1,000 asset limit had not been raised since 1981), particularly affecting poor persons who tried to own a car;

- time limits or work requirements;

- expansion of requirements to participate in JOBS;

- Medicaid changes that extend or expand Medicaid coverage for AFDC families in transition to work;

- required school attendance.

Even the names of state projects demonstrate their new intent. In Massachusetts, the Department of Public Welfare became the Department of Transitional Assistance. The Virginia Independence Program, the New Jersey Family Development Program, and Wisconsin's Work Not Welfare program are other examples.

In early 1996, Clinton announced that states would be required to submit annual plans for keeping teen mothers on welfare in school. Previously, states could apply for waivers to test programs of this nature. Clinton's announcement meant that all states would be free to develop such programs, and states would also have to show the federal government what they were doing to meet this goal. Stated Clinton, "State by state, we are building a welfare system that demands work, requires responsibility, and protects our children."

# Welfare Programs Today

In 1995 and 1996 it was difficult to pick up a newspaper or turn on television news without finding a story about welfare reform. In 1994, this was true of health care reform, although ambitious federal legislation in that area failed to pass Congress. There was a good chance that the welfare reform story was one with images of poor unmarried women with children, receiving monthly cash payments under the AFDC program. Maybe it was a story about teen mothers. Or perhaps it was a story about out-of-wedlock births, or proposals to prevent additional payments when poor women have additional children. These examples raise many issues, but it is often difficult to figure out how they fit together. As is frequently the case with highly controversial issues, the noise and heat of the debate obscure other ongoing activity away from the cameras.

The welfare reform policy debate relies on the term "welfare" as a substitute for identifying a much larger number of programs than AFDC alone. AFDC represents only 1 percent of federal expenditures and only 3.2 percent of state expenditures, as of 1994, although it is linked to other more costly programs and forms of assistance, including food stamps and Medicaid. The use of such a shorthand term is not unusual in the media, but it does obscure the more complicated facts at work. It also relies on what has been characterized as "the nearly universal views of Americans. No other major social institution evokes such hostility from its clients, who find it punitive and degrading, from liberals, who see it as hopelessly inadequate and full of disincentives, or from conservatives, who believe it is overly generous and rewards bad behavior. . . . [Welfare reform] (including many of the state initiatives in the early 1990s) has been as much about improving poor people by changing their behavior as about helping them with food, housing, or cash" (Katz 1995).

Dozens of separate programs exist to serve low-income people; some aspects of the debate have embraced over 300 programs that give any form of assistance (including student loans, for instance). The primary assistance programs came into being over a period of years, beginning with the passage of the Social Security Act in 1935. These assistance programs were created by the U.S. Congress at different times during the last 60 years. At different points during those 60 years, different individuals were members of the Senate and House of Representatives, under various presidential administrations. Different issues held sway in the major political parties and in the public's mind at the points when these programs were first suggested and later when they passed Congress and were signed into law by the president. Different social patterns—such as expectations for women's roles—also shape responses. These economic, political, and social realities, which differ both at specific times (the 1950s and the 1980s for example) and over the period of all 60 years, are also important to recognize when examining a question that is both enduring and complex in human community: how should inequities in access to or distribution of basic necessities be addressed? The answer to that question has varied depending on social trends of the moment, as well as the economic health of the community or nation at the time. Policy responses have not been limited by these factors alone.

This book is premised on a definition of welfare and welfare reform that includes a range of low-income assistance programs beyond AFDC, but not the entire universe of programs providing aid of any sort. Because the debate revolves so closely around work and worthiness, only a tight core of programs is examined here. While this book recognizes a public policy debate that accelerated during the early 1990s and uses AFDC as a symbol of all assistance, it also recognizes that dramatic change in assistance programs for low-income people began much earlier and will continue no matter how the federal legislative debate ends. For instance, at the state and county level in many states, cash assistance programs known as General Assistance (GA), General Relief, or Home Relief exist to provide temporary cash payments to individuals with disabilities. Just as the AFDC program is best known as a source of cash assistance for single women with children, the GA programs are best known as those that provide public benefits to single poor men. However, the AFDC program has less visible components that provide assistance to two-parent families. The "single mother" characteristic of AFDC is equated with women who have never married and have borne all their children outside of marriage. Although one goal of some welfare proposals is to reduce out-of-wedlock births, poverty—not marital status—is the determinant of eligibility for AFDC.

# What Is Welfare?

Understanding the welfare programs themselves can help sort out some of the opposing viewpoints that are at the center of the welfare debate. To do this, it is helpful to understand the basic categories of assistance that are rooted at the federal level. The programs generally included in the welfare debate are: income assistance (such as AFDC, General Assistance, Social Security); medical care (Medicaid); food and nutrition assistance (food stamps; Women, Infants, and Children [WIC] nutrition program; school breakfasts and lunches); housing assistance (public housing and other housing help); education and training (Job Training Partnership Act, Head Start); and other minor programs for low-income people (legal services and energy assistance).

# Who Receives Welfare?

The characteristics of recipients of assistance are another important area to examine. We all have stereotypes and images of people. Are they accurate? If we learn facts about welfare programs or their beneficiaries that differ from our initial ideas, does this new information change how we think about the debate? Do the policy ideas being debated in Congress have a direct relation to what we know about women who receive AFDC, for example? Finally, it is important to look at what public opinion says about programs, their recipients, and the actions of policymakers. All of these factors help define the debate.

AFDC began as a successor program to state pensions for widowed mothers. These women were considered extremely worthy recipients of public aid. Society did not want them to go to work in order to raise their children. Economic, social, and political changes in the years since then have been enormous. How has this affected the AFDC program? According to one analyst:

> A quarter-century after its inception, AFDC remained a relatively modest and obscure program. In 1960, less than one child in twenty-five received AFDC in a typical month, although more than one child in four (26.9 percent) would have been considered poor by today's standards. In consequence, only about 13 percent of all poor children received AFDC.The typical grant at that time was about $108 per month. Total expenditures on benefits of a little over $1 billion went to some 800,000 families.
>
> By 1992, however, more than one child in eight and over 60 percent of all poor children were receiving AFDC in any given month. The program provided benefits to a monthly average of almost 5 million families (14.2 million individuals, two-thirds of which are children). The AFDC caseload now represents about 5 percent of the total resident U.S. population and about 14 percent of all children.
>
> What had been a small and uncontroversial provision of the Social Security Act gradually became a symbol for all that is wrong with the welfare state. In effect, the program persisted as the world changed. The composition of the caseload was transformed

from one that easily evoked sympathy and concern to one that generated apathy at best, antipathy at the worst. In the early 1940s, there were as many widows on ADC as there were women who were divorced, separated, or unmarried. The number of widows on the rolls dropped by a third by the end of that decade and constituted about 7 percent of the caseload by the early 1960s. Second, societal expectations about the role of women changed dramatically. Following World War II, less than 20 percent of mothers worked; now two-thirds of mothers with children are in the labor force. Third, a demographic earthquake has occurred in recent decades. The number of children in single-parent homes rose from about 8 percent in 1960 to over 25 percent today. Births to unmarried women increased from about 5 percent of all births in 1960 to 18 percent in 1980 to about 30 percent at present. Demographers estimate that over half of all children born today will spend some of their childhood in a single-parent home. Finally, poverty among children has worsened. In 1992, 14.6 million children lived in poverty, yet in 1978 the number of poor children was less than 10 million (Corbett 1994/1995).

According to the Census Bureau, about 14 million people were receiving AFDC in 1995. This included 3.8 million mothers age 15 to 44; 500,000 mothers age 45 and over; 300,000 fathers living with dependent children; and 9.7 million children. Nearly half of women on AFDC have never been married. The average mother on AFDC gave birth at age 20, compared to age 23 for women not on AFDC. The average AFDC family has 2.6 children, compared to 2.1 for families not on AFDC. Almost half of AFDC mothers did not complete high school, compared to 15 percent of women not on AFDC. More white women of childbearing age receive AFDC than black or Hispanic women, but black and Hispanic women receive AFDC in disproportionate numbers. About 63.5 percent of AFDC recipients live in private-market housing; only about 9 percent live in public housing. About 87 percent receive food stamps.

About 14 percent of recipients have been on AFDC for more than three years. About 32 percent have received benefits for one to three years, and 34 percent have received benefits for less than one year.

# Do Welfare Mothers Want to Work?

What about the idea that women who receive AFDC can't or don't want to work? A study of work in the lives of women on AFDC was released in 1995. This study, by the Institute for Women's Policy Research, was based on information from 1984, 1986, 1987, and 1988. It examined women who were single mothers for one year of a two-year period and who had received AFDC for at least two months during the two years. The findings included these:

On average, women in the sample were single for 23 of 24 months and received AFDC for 18 months. The resulting sample included 1,181 single welfare mothers, with an average of 2.1 children apiece, representing 80 percent of all adults and 81 percent of all children receiving AFDC.

More than seven of ten AFDC recipients in the sample were in the labor force, either working or looking for work.

Three-quarters of those who received AFDC combined this income source with earnings from low-wage and unstable jobs and income from family members.

Fifty-eight percent of the women who combined work and welfare with other sources, including income from other family members, achieved family incomes above the poverty line, as opposed to only 2 percent of the welfare families that relied on welfare alone (Spalter-Roth, Burr, Hartmann, and Shaw 1995).

# State Welfare Programs

The General Assistance (GA) program is a cash assistance program in some states and counties. It serves many single disabled persons. In 1991, Michigan took the first of what were to be many similar state actions that began welfare reform on the nonfederal level. Of the 27 states with GA programs, 17 of them cut their programs in 1991–92. Michigan completely eliminated GA coverage. GA provided $160 per month to more than 80,000 people when it was ended in Michigan. People on GA also received food stamps and medical coverage. According to a 1994 report on the Michigan program,

A basic descriptive analysis of the General Assistance population from the 1991 caseload (prior to the program's end) yielded very little confidence that recipients would be able to replace GA income through private means. Some of the findings included the following:

two of five recipients were over age forty;

only half had a high school diploma;

half of the cases were in Wayne County/Detroit, one of the highest unemployment areas and concentrated minority poverty areas of the state (Danziger and Kossoudji 1994).

# Background of the Recent Debate

Running throughout the reform debate has been the central question of whether government has an obligation to the poor. If it does, what is that obligation? Increasingly in recent years, the notion that government should help, or even that an individual has a "right" to be helped in circumstances of poverty, has meshed with a new standard that would make that right not unquestioned but reciprocal. According to this viewpoint, a right to basics such as food, income, and shelter ought to be exchanged for "responsibility" in having children, in seeking employment when possible, and in getting off assistance programs as soon as feasible. Many recent proposals to reform welfare programs would, in fact, end the right or entitlement to assistance and leave many key decisions (such as who to help, how much, and for how long) to individual states. One reason these changes represent such a dramatic shift is that the entitlement to assistance has long been coupled with a belief that a federal standard for assistance was necessary to ensure that states did not try to do as little as possible for their poorest residents.

It has long been a basis of federal policy that federal resources, wisely used, can transform lives for the better. But 1995 saw Republicans on Capitol Hill—and many Democrats—proposing a tough new vision of social welfare in which it is the poor who have an obligation to society. Federal legislators, however, have mainly been following the lead of the states, which moved first to change welfare recipients' behavior. For instance, a number of states took steps in the early 1990s through the waiver process to end the practice of increasing a family's AFDC benefit when a mother already receiving welfare has an additional child. This is referred to as a "child exclusion" provision.

Personal responsibility and family values are the political slogans of the debate, embodied in an array of proposals to discourage certain forms of behavior (especially out-of-wedlock births) and to cure "dependency" on aid programs by limiting help. Fostering self-sufficiency, not providing compassion, has been defined as the goal of federal action. Indeed, the idea that assistance programs are a compassionate means of assistance has been questioned by those who believe that aid without demands results in dependence and long-term reliance on welfare programs, rather than self-reliance. Thus, these critics argue, these forms of "compassion" create dependency without end and are misguided in their approach. Better to demand efforts toward employment and education, establish specific time limits for aid, and penalize such undesired behavior as having additional children, failing to cooperate in establishing the paternity of children, or encouraging births to teen mothers. The underlying notion of federal government spending for social programs, which has been one of the distinguishing features of traditional liberal politics, has been called into question by the increasing fiscal pressure of the federal budget deficit.

While much recent debate about welfare reform has underscored behavioral issues of personal responsibility related to parenting, these public policy dilemmas are more complex than not. They reflect an array of forces at work in our history as well as in our society and our communities. Their rise to prominence now also coincides with other political, social, and economic developments, including rising program costs, growing caseloads, and criticisms of program design.

Both federal and state concerns have fueled the welfare reform debate of the early 1990s. One goal at work is the creation of an ideal assistance system that would be easy to understand, simple to administer, and reward the behavior it seeks to promote. Another goal is to eliminate what are viewed as incongruities in the present system, such as penalizing people for getting a job or marrying. Virtually all parties want to establish clear rewards for those who work and create stable families. Similarly, virtually everyone agrees that major improvement in child support enforcement is critical.

The debate has largely unfolded in the U.S. Congress and in the individual state legislatures. These developments have in turn been communicated to the public through print and broadcast media, including newspapers and radio and television news. Because of the recent proliferation in the use of electronic technologies, information related to the debate (including legislative proposals) has been available via computer.

But just because modern communications have spread the debate broadly does not mean that all of the issues involved are new. This is far from true. In fact, observing the debate closely can prove even more confusing. Discussion involves terms such as "culture of poverty," "the social contract," and "the underclass." Orphanages have been suggested as an antidote to life in a poor family. One day's news might show a legislator decrying the number of unmarried women having children. The next week's welfare reform coverage might show members of Congress in a tense discussion with governors about complex details of how each state will receive its share of federal funding. Are both of these images about welfare reform? Is either of them? These are just two examples of the many issues that have become part of the welfare reform debate. Others include:

1. Should federal and state government (or cities, in some cases), on behalf of society in general, provide assistance (cash benefits, services, etc.) of any sort to those in need (however defined)? Do we owe this to others, via government?
2. If so, should this assistance be viewed as a right by those in need or those delivering it?
3. If so, should this right be tied to specific desired outcomes or behaviors for those receiving the assistance?
4. What kind of assistance should be provided?
5. How long should assistance be available? Should there be time limits on the receipt of assistance?
6. Who should be eligible for assistance? Should there be restrictions on the receipt of assistance by teens, or people who are legal or illegal residents of the United States?
7. Should the provision of assistance be tied to other goals, such as fiscal savings, reductions in births, transition to employment?
8. What are the desired fiscal and programmatic results for the states? Should states receive federal funds based on prior expenditures, population patterns, poverty population, meeting specific goals? Should states receive

funds based on past funding, with or without a requirement that they expend any state funds, or the same
amount of funds?
9. What are the desired results for recipients of assistance?
Should the results of spending be the reason to halt or
change other program goals? For instance, if large numbers of children are inadequately nourished, should a
program be altered to make more people eligible for
assistance?

The fundamental questions are not new. At least some of
what each opposing side in the debate says seems to strike a
chord. But that does not mean that solutions can be arrived at
easily. As one observer stated when the welfare overhaul and the
budget debate were at their most pitched: "The plot is so convo-
luted, the developments are so incremental and the characters
seem so agitated when they speak that even avid followers of the
political script often have trouble figuring out what is going on
and who is at fault . . ." (Rosenbaum 1995).

The widespread fiscal pressures facing both state and federal government led several states to begin welfare reductions
targeted at General Assistance (GA) programs in the early 1990s.
Some states entirely dismantled their programs. While the notion of fiscal necessity has been the underpinning of such
changes, the beneficiaries of GA have traditionally had access to
no other income assistance, receive relatively low benefits, and
do not represent a constituency with the ability to combat such
cuts. One analyst has characterized the pros and cons of federal
block grant involvement as including the following factors: entitlements versus caps; distribution issues; federal control versus
local discretion; administrative efficiencies or inefficiencies; cost-
sharing or matching requirements; and variations in funding
(Wolfe 1995).

Changes passed in the federal Supplemental Security Income (SSI) program in 1994 and 1996 provide a good example of
federal goals and roles. SSI pays cash benefits to poor people
with disabilities. Many recipients of local GA benefits are actually waiting to qualify for federal SSI benefits. One form of disability for which a person may receive assistance is based on
alcohol and/or drug addiction. During the late 1980s and early
1990s, the benefit payment rolls for this form of disability grew
rapidly. Media reports highlighted cases in which individuals receiving addiction-related assistance were still actively using

drugs or alcohol, thus leading to the conclusion that the benefits were supporting the continuing active use of drugs or alcohol. Changes in 1994 to limit the duration of these benefits were followed by 1996 changes that will eliminate these benefits entirely in 1997.

# Different Viewpoints

What is the nature of the opposing viewpoints in the welfare reform debate? A starting point is to analyze the changing opinion about assistance that has led to the debate itself. According to one analyst, this shift can be described as follows.

> Over the past decade (at least) we have witnessed major changes in the conceptual and political consensus that supports public assistance policy in the United States and, in consequence, the nature of that policy. The evolving consensus includes renewed emphasis on the obligation of recipients of public assistance to seek employment and behave in ways consistent with an independent lifestyle[, and] reorientation of welfare operations from an entitlement orientation to an emphasis upon the transition of recipients from welfare dependence to self-support.
>
> . . . Conservatives believe that AFDC destroys initiative and discourages work and marriage. Liberals argue that it offers inadequate benefits while robbing individuals of their dignity and self-esteem. Recipients feel degraded and trapped by a system that offers no reward for their efforts to be self-sufficient and that gives them little control over their lives. Taxpayers increasingly decry spending what appears to be an increasing amount on a program from which they see few positive results. Few, it would appear, defend the system. A 1992 national survey found that nine of ten Americans believed that the welfare system should be changed. This opinion was held by blacks (81 percent) and whites (92 percent), conservatives (92 percent) and liberals (89 percent), and the more affluent (93 percent) and the less affluent (87 percent). Republicans and Democrats responded in like fashion (both at 89 percent) (Corbett 1994/1995).

The profile of a welfare recipient promoted by this view is of a single mother with many children, who is probably sexually promiscuous, had additional children for the additional increase in benefits that results, is poorly educated, is disinterested in work opportunities, and is probably black or Hispanic. In the case of General Assistance programs, the average recipient is presented as being an able-bodied, employable, minority male who could work but doesn't.

Conservatives are generally opposed to what is seen as "big government." This includes increased federal spending, federal standards and regulations in programs, and the idea that the federal government (rather than the market economy, for instance) should be relied on to solve problems. It also includes federal oversight of state actions.

Some believe that punitive policies will motivate change on the part of program beneficiaries, since, according to this view, if given the choice these individuals will choose a monthly check with no or few strings attached instead of work. Ending the cash assistance provided to such people and requiring work is viewed as the only way to change the status quo. The conservative view of welfare reform can best be summed up in the proposals of the Contract with America, which included three major points on welfare reform: reduction of illegitimacy and establishment of measures to promote that goal; work requirements for AFDC; and increased flexibility to state governments in the operation of welfare programs. In addition, the conservative view includes reducing divorce and increasing marriage among women who have had children out of wedlock.

Liberal advocates for AFDC counter that the average welfare recipient is a woman facing multiple barriers posed by gender, race, age, and single parenthood. She is trying to raise children with below-poverty-level benefits. She should have access to education, training, and employment at good wages if she is to leave welfare. She should have adequate child care and health care for her family. She should not be punished for failures of the economy to provide good jobs or her own desire to remain at home with her children and be provided for. Liberal Democrats, long the supporters of the assistance programs, have trod carefully in the debate. They desire not to be seen as encouraging the behavior their opponents portray as the inevitable result of welfare, but they don't want to defend what the public seems unprepared to accept any longer. Yet they are still constrained by 60 years of political legacy. Thus, some Democrats proposed reforms of their own, starting with the Democratic presidential candidate in 1992. Rather than focus attention on the behavior of individuals, liberal proponents of existing programs suggest that increased government assistance can advance goals of work and independence through several specific means.

## Looking Ahead

The debate about welfare reform is not concluded. While there have been periods of stalemate in political action in the Congress and the executive branch, there have also been periodic intense negotiations among governors and other officials. Coalitions have formed around fiscal and social policy issues, trying to craft proposals that had a chance of passage or might change the debate. According to one analyst, however the debate is resolved, some fundamental change emphasizing work will be achieved. As a result of that change:

> . . . Based on the experience of the most successful programs that have adopted [a labor force attachment model], it is reasonable to expect that as a result:
>
> An increased number of program entrants will enter employment, but often into low wage jobs;
>
> A number of participants will enter into jobs which do not last;
>
> A number of participants will not find unsubsidized employment, despite fully complying with program rules; and
>
> A number of participants will not fully comply with program rules (Greenberg 1996).

Many structural issues are raised by the debate, but not necessarily resolved. Another analyst suggests that these issues can be categorized as fiscal effects, political effects, and institutional/programmatic effects (Lurie 1996). Fiscal issues include questions about how states will change benefit levels and eligibility criteria, as well as whether states will provide any safety net programs for those in need. Political issues include the effect of block grants on state leadership (both legislative and executive branches), the roles and political alignment of special interests, and the relation of all these parties to the federal government. Institutional and programmatic issues include the shift from emphasis on education and training to jobs, the possible reorganization of systems of service delivery, enforcement of federally imposed work requirements, and the role of private social service organizations.

A core issue to be addressed will be the influence on the child welfare system. The suggestion of reviving orphanages for poor children received extensive media coverage in the early welfare reform debate. According to one expert, the issue can be summarized as follows:

> Child maltreatment reports are the most concrete indicator of "demand" for child welfare services; they must be responded to by child welfare authorities and they are the entry point to substitute care. The number of these reports nationally has tripled since 1981, reaching approximately 3 million last year. The deluge of child abuse reports in an era of stable or declining resources has placed child welfare systems under great stress. Several child welfare jurisdictions have lawsuits pending against them owing to their apparent failure to carry out basic child welfare service functions, and others are already operating under court decrees.
>
> The vast majority of children in substitute care come from single-parent homes; about half come from AFDC-eligible families. Poverty is the best predictor of child neglect—the primary reason for child placement—as well as a strong predictor of other forms of child maltreatment. Welfare reform efforts which eliminate or significantly reduce economic support for poor families will lead to an unpredictable increase in child maltreatment, and a corresponding increase in demand for child welfare services, including foster care (Courtney 1995).

With new legislation signed in August 1996, states were able to move immediately to revise their welfare programs. With the start of the new fiscal year on 1 October 1996, the federal assistance guarantee ended and food stamp benefits were reduced. In July 1997, new federal requirements for cash assistance programs

will take effect. States have until then to meet the new requirements so they can begin their block grant programs at that time.
Noncitizens receiving food stamps and Supplemental Security
Income (SSI) began losing their benefits after the signing of the
new law and once their cases are reviewed.

Emerging program measures will stress participation requirements and penalties for noncompliance. The structure and
distribution of program funds will underscore the tensions between the federal and state governments, as well as between
states facing different issues. Government will seek to reduce
waste, fraud, and abuse in programs and lower administrative
costs through measures using new technologies, such as electronic benefits and fingerprinting. The trend to reduce disparities
created by assistance for unemployed people will be the focus of
further action. Reduced federal funding, the end of guaranteed
assistance, the actions of the states, and the turn of public opinion to support of work as a priority for recipients of assistance
will be the biggest influences on the next phase of policy.

# References

Corbett, Thomas. "Welfare Block Grants: Concepts, Controversies, and
Context." Forum on Welfare Block Grants: Advantages and Disadvantages. *Focus* 17, 1 (Summer 1995). Institute for Research on Poverty: University of Wisconsin-Madison.

————. "Changing the Culture of Welfare." *Focus* 16, 2 (Winter
1994/1995). Institute for Research on Poverty: University of Wisconsin-
Madison.

Courtney, Mark. "The Federal Role in Child Welfare Services." *Focus* 17,
1 (1995). Institute for Research on Poverty: University of Wisconsin-
Madison.

Danziger, Sandra, and Sherrie A. Kossoudji. "What Happened to General Assistance Recipients in Michigan?" *Focus* 16, 2 (Winter 1994/1995).
Institute for Research on Poverty: University of Wisconsin-Madison.

Greenberg, Mark. "Welfare Reform in An Uncertain Environment."
Paper presented at "Planning a State/Local Welfare Strategy After the
104th Congress," a conference organized by the Carnegie Corporation
Project on Confronting the New Politics of Child and Family Policies in
the United States. February 1996.

Katz, Michael B. *Improving Poor People.* Princeton, NJ: Princeton University Press. 1995.

Lurie, Irene. "The Impact of Welfare Reform: More Questions than Answers." Symposium: American Federalism Today, *Rockefeller Institute Bulletin*. 1996.

*New York Times*. 29 January 1992. A-17.

Rosenbaum, David E. "Nuts and Bolts of Gridlock: A Primer on the Shutdown." *New York Times*. 30 December 1995.

Spalter-Roth, Roberta, Beverly Burr, Heidi Hartmann, and Lois B. Shaw. "Welfare That Works: The Working Lives of AFDC Recipients." A Report to the Ford Foundation by the Institute for Women's Policy Research. *Focus* 17, 2 (Fall/Winter 1995). Institute for Research on Poverty: University of Wisconsin-Madison.

Trattner, Walter I. *From Poor Law to Welfare State*. New York: Free Press. 1974.

Wolfe, Barbara. "Issues Involved in Federalism." Forum on Welfare Block Grants: Advantages and Disadvantages. *Focus* 17, 1 ( Summer 1995). Institute for Research on Poverty: University of Wisconsin–Madison.

# Chronology 2

Events in the debate about welfare reform should be viewed in the context of both the foundations of the programs in U.S. history and in their relationship to broader political factors, such as the 1994 congressional elections and the 1996 presidential campaign. The historical context provides a perspective on how much change is proposed. The more contemporary political factors also influence the debate because the 1994 congressional elections swept many Republican candidates into office under the aegis of the Contract with America, which promised reform at every level of government. Additionally, key congressional leaders in the welfare reform debate have also sometimes become aspirants for the presidency in the 1996 elections. As such, their actions in the welfare reform debate and other arenas also reflect their efforts to seek support and take positions that make them more appealing to voters.

Below are outlined some key events from the last 60 years of federal social programs, as well as key developments in the welfare reform debate since 1992, which marked the public commencement of efforts to "end welfare as we know it." The events of the contemporary debate are presented in some detail, but they are not meant to reflect every development in the debate of the 1990s. The details of proposals, positions, and politics emphasize or illustrate the primary themes throughout the formation of public policy in this area.

## Significant Events in the History of Federal Welfare Programs

1932    Three years after the start of the Great Depression, millions of Americans have lost their jobs, their savings, their homes, and their land. Franklin Delano Roosevelt, in accepting the Democratic presidential nomination and taking over the White House from Republican Herbert Hoover, states: "The country needs, and unless I mistake its temper, the country demands bold, persistent experimentation. It is common sense to take a method and try it. If it fails try another. But above all, try something."

1933    The Federal Emergency Relief Act is signed into law to make available to the states $500 million in grants for emergency unemployment relief. Responsibility for administering the new funds rests with state and local government.

1935    In January President Roosevelt charges Congress with creating a workable social security program. Such a program becomes law in August. It is aimed at preventing destitution through contributory social insurance and public assistance, old-age insurance and pensions for the needy aged, unemployment insurance, and assistance to dependent mothers with children, the crippled, and the blind.

1936    Governor Alf Landon of Kansas runs for president against Franklin Roosevelt. Landon attacks Roosevelt's New Deal programs of social spending, proposing instead that relief be turned over to the states and cities. (In 1994, Landon's daughter, Senator Nancy Landon Kassebaum, becomes chair of the Senate Labor and

Human Resources Committee, which will consider welfare reform that shifts spending and governance back to the states.)

1945    In April President Franklin Roosevelt dies. He is succeeded by Vice President Harry Truman, who promises to continue Roosevelt's policies.

In November, Truman sends a message to Congress regarding national compulsory health insurance. The plan would be financed through payroll deductions.

1947    In May President Truman sends recommendations to Congress on the establishment of a compulsory health insurance program.

1957    In August a Senate committee approves a proposal for the federal and state governments to share in paying the medical expenses of needy aged people.

1961    Democratic President John F. Kennedy states in his inaugural address that "the hand of hope must be extended to the poor and oppressed."

1962    In March social scientist Michael Harrington's book about American poverty, *The Other America*, is released.

1963    In August clergyman and civil rights leader Reverend Martin Luther King, Jr., leads over 200,000 people in a march at the Lincoln Memorial, where he gives a speech called "I Have a Dream." It is a historic event in the civil rights movement of the 1960s, which has drawn the nation's attention to poverty and inequality.

1964    Democratic President Lyndon B. Johnson calls on Congress to enact a 13-point program to declare "unconditional war on poverty" in the United States. The Economic Opportunity Act passed later that year creates VISTA, the Job Corps, Head Start, community action programs, and other programs.

1965    President Lyndon Johnson signs into law the Social Security Act amendments that create the Medicare and Medicaid programs.

1968    The Kerner Commission, reporting on its investigation of major civil rights riots in urban areas in 1967, announces that earlier civil rights gains have done little to improve the quality of life for poor urban black people.

1969    Republican President Richard Nixon calls for drastic change in the nation's welfare system, proposing the Family Assistance Plan, which would alter programs unchanged since the 1930s. The Nixon plan proposes that every unemployed family of four would receive at least $1,600 a year from the federal government. This assistance is designed to provide the difference between low wages and what is required to live above the poverty line. Working poor people would be allowed to keep more of their pay under the plan, and all able-bodied people (except mothers with small children) would be required to work or be in a job-training program. In a plan called the "new federalism" the program would eventually be turned over to the states. The proposal provokes immediate controversy and ultimately fails.

1972    Congress creates the Supplemental Security Income program (SSI) to provide a cash income to poor elderly and disabled adults unable to work. Needy children are included to help their families with extra expenses resulting from a child's disabilities.

1975    Massachusetts begins to dismantle its General Relief program.

1982    Pennsylvania moves to make major reforms in its General Assistance program. Pennsylvania Governor Richard Thornburgh says he believes the labor market and self-reliance are preferable to welfare assistance.

1986    Arkansas, Louisiana, and Oklahoma begin steps that will dismantle General Assistance programs over the next two years.

1988    The U.S. Congress passes the Family Support Act, welfare reform legislation that creates the JOBS program, after more than a year of effort.

# Significant Events in the Current Debate

1992    Democratic presidential contender Governor Bill Clinton of Arkansas pledges during his campaign to "end welfare as we know it" if elected.

Michigan Governor John Engler moves to eliminate the General Assistance program in state.

1993    A Tufts University study based on the latest Census Bureau poverty data projects that 52 percent of black children and 49.2 percent of Hispanic children in the United States will live in poverty by 2010.

House Republicans announce their welfare plan on 10 November. The plan has 160 cosponsors, and its authors claim it will save $20 billion over five years. It offers a massive workfare program, strict sanction requirements, paternity determination rules, state options for a wide variety of measures to control individual behavior, expanded and expedited waiver procedures, elimination of welfare benefits for immigrants, an "entitlement cap" on low-income entitlement programs, and a block grant of the food stamp programs with nine other nutrition programs, among them the Women, Infants, and Children (WIC) nutrition program.

Several accounts of the efforts of the Clinton administration's Working Group on Welfare Reform, Family Support, and Independence are publicized. The *New York Times* reports that the Working Group's proposal builds on the Family Support Act rather than replacing it. It calls for improvements in the child support enforcement system, proposes offering education and training opportunities to noncustodial parents, and suggests creating a system to ensure advance payment of the Earned Income Tax Credit.

1994    In January, the Clinton administration's Working Group on Welfare Reform, Family Support, and Independence completes a preliminary draft of its welfare proposals. President Bill Clinton's commitment to impose a two-year time limit on cash assistance is a central principle

1994
cont.

of the draft proposal. He features welfare reform as part of his State of the Union address on 25 January.

The *Washington Post* reports that Working Group members have discussed cutting public assistance programs to legal immigrants to finance the administration's welfare reform initiative. Reports in the *New York Times* indicate that a proposal to tax welfare benefits, food stamps, and housing assistance has also been considered.

The Center on Social Welfare Policy and Law issues a report on what happened to former General Assistance (GA) recipients in Ohio, Pennsylvania, Michigan, and Illinois, after their states slashed or eliminated their GA programs. Most of the "employable" people cut from GA were unable to secure jobs in the following one to two years. For those who did find work, it was typically low-wage, temporary, and/or part-time. The cuts also caused significant increases in hunger and homelessness among those dropped.

New Democrats in the House of Representatives approve and send to the administration a set of basic principles on welfare reform. The statement cautions against arbitrary time limits and advocates placing welfare recipients in jobs that pay a living wage.

In April, a new Republican bill sponsored by 18 members of the Senate and 28 House members is announced by Senator Lauch Faircloth (R-NC) and Congressman Jim Talent (R-MO). The measure focuses on an issue supported by social scientist Charles Murray: the elimination of welfare benefits as the primary means for eliminating out-of-wedlock births. Under the bill, not only Aid to Families with Dependent Children (AFDC), but also food stamps and housing assistance would be eliminated for young unmarried mothers. The measure includes a family cap or "child exclusion" provision that denies not only the AFDC increase normally available to families, but also precludes food stamps for that child. In addition, the bill puts caps on overall welfare spending, folds a large number of social programs into a capped block grant to states, and emphasizes workfare.

The *New York Times* reports that a confidential memo presented to President Clinton outlines the possibility that his welfare overhaul plan could add $58 billion to the nation's costs over 10 years. The memo also states that the use of the two-year time limit for benefits could result in increased homelessness.

In a letter to President Clinton, eight Senate Republicans break with some members of their own party on welfare reform. The senators sign a letter applauding Clinton's determination to reform the welfare and health care systems and stating that the focus of welfare reform must remain on children, who make up two-thirds of all AFDC recipients.

President Clinton announces his welfare reform bill, the Work and Responsibility Act of 1994.

President Clinton speaks to the National Governors' Association in July on four aspects of welfare reform, emphasizing (1) the importance of the Family Support Act—the president insists that any new welfare reform initiative should build on the 1988 legislation, which he helped craft; (2) that billions of dollars of child support go uncollected every year—a factor he says drives people on to welfare; (3) that states play a vital role as experimenters for trials of new welfare programs; and (4) that he supports time limits for welfare, reiterating his campaign promise and asking the governors to "support the notion that there ought to be some period after which we end welfare as we know it."

In September, more than 300 Republican candidates for Congress gather to unveil what they call a "Republican Contract with America. . . . A Campaign Promise Is One Thing. A Signed Contract Is Quite Another." The Republicans present ten bills that they would introduce during the first 100 days of the 104th Congress if and "when Republicans become the majority of the House of Representatives." The Republicans provide a brief summary of the welfare section of the Personal Responsibility Act, which would "[d]iscourage illegitimacy and teen pregnancy by prohibiting welfare to minor mothers

1994
cont.

and denying increased AFDC for additional children while on welfare, cut spending for welfare programs, and enact a tough two-years-and-out provision with work requirements to promote individual responsibility." More specifically, it denies benefits to out-of-wedlock children born to minor teen mothers. States also would have the option to deny benefits to older, 18- to 20-year-old mothers and their out-of-wedlock children. Further, there would be no housing subsidies or benefits for such families and the food stamp program would no longer exist for all families.

A news article suggests that welfare reform legislation will not move beyond a House subcommittee markup this year. The article quotes a spokesperson for acting Ways and Means Chairman Sam Gibbons (D-FL), saying Gibbons is "concerned that there isn't enough time to do it properly" in full committee or on the floor.

The Subcommittee on Human Resources of the Education and Labor Committee hears testimony focusing on the relationship between child care and welfare reform. At the hearing, the General Accounting Office (GAO) presented recent research showing that (1) child care subsidies can dramatically affect whether low-income women work; (2) despite significant increases in federal child care funding in recent years, only a small percentage of the need is being filled; (3) the fragmentation of the child care funding streams results in unintended gaps in services; and (4) as states experience more pressure to provide child care for welfare recipients, their support for working poor families declines.

Twenty-three members of the House Ways and Means Committee ask the Department of Health and Human Services (HHS) to respond to 20 questions regarding the administration's welfare bill. In a letter to HHS Secretary Donna Shalala, the members write: "We share the President's goal of basing our nation's welfare system on values that Americans hold most dearly—work, family and responsibility. . . . However, the legislation has numerous and complex features which ultimately will help to determine its effectiveness."

The November 1994 elections put Republicans in control of the U.S. Congress for the first time in years. Freshman House Republicans are elected after signing a Contract with America that includes proposals in ten substantive areas, including welfare reform. The Contract's specific welfare proposal, called the Personal Responsibility Act, would deny welfare to millions, including permanent denial of benefits to teen mothers and legal immigrants, and impose harsh provisions on others. One highly publicized element is the proposal to fund orphanages with welfare dollars.

According to a new study of the 50 states and the District of Columbia released by the Center on Social Welfare Policy and Law, benefits under the nation's largest welfare program, AFDC, have reached their lowest point in over 20 years. As a result, poor families are even less able than they were in past years to meet their children's basic needs for food, clothing, shelter, school supplies, and household goods. In all 50 states and the District of Columbia, AFDC benefits, even when combined with food stamps, leave families well below the poverty line.

1995    In January, Republican governors and members of Congress outline their welfare reform plan, which would block grant food and nutrition programs, cash welfare, child care aid, social services, and child welfare and child abuse funds. Some 133 federal programs with current appropriations of almost $78 billion would be included in the five new programs.

The Personal Responsibility Act of 1995 is introduced in the House of Representatives. The bill is sponsored by Congressman Clay Shaw (R-FL), chair of the Human Resources Subcommittee of the House Ways and Means Committee, and 111 other Republican members of the House. The AFDC provisions in the bill, known as H.R. 4, are largely identical to those in the draft version released in late 1994.

As the first portion of the House Republican welfare plan emerges from the Ways and Means Subcommittee on Human Resources, Senator Daniel Patrick Moynihan (D-NY) launches an attack on it, asserting that "the answer to our problems is not to turn children out into the street." Moynihan has long been recognized as an expert on welfare and social security.

President Clinton proposes a 90 cent increase in the minimum wage. The rate would increase over two years to $5.15 per hour.

The House will vote on welfare reform without considering the nation's largest entitlement program, Medicaid, says a spokesperson for the Republican Governors' Association Medicaid Task Force. The Personal Responsibility Act, H.R. 4 (HR1214), is approved by the House of Representatives. The vote, 234 to 199, is largely along party lines. H.R. 4 eliminates a number of essential low-income "entitlement" (matching grant) programs and converts them into block grants. Also, it includes enormous cutbacks in the food stamp program and Supplemental Security Income. The House Rules Committee does not permit fundamental amendments to be debated on the floor. President Clinton outlines the administration's position on the House bill in a letter to Speaker of the House Newt Gingrich (R-GA), in which he writes, "When people just get cut off without going to work, that's not welfare reform."

The Children's Defense Fund releases a report attacking the House of Representatives for slashing $40 billion from children's programs and using the savings to fund an "unnecessary defense build-up," a capital gains tax cut for the "richest 1 percent of Americans," and a tax cut for the "richest 13 percent of the elderly."

House Republicans add to their welfare reform proposals a provision to pay cash bonuses to states that reduce out-of-wedlock births, regardless of whether the births or abortions are to women receiving public assistance. Republicans describe this in the debate as the "illegitimacy ratio" proposal. They view this as a crisis of out-of-wedlock births nationally.

John Cardinal O'Connor states that the welfare reform legislation currently under consideration in the Contract with America is "immoral in its virtually inevitable consequences" of increasing abortions.

A draft Republican governors' welfare reform bill is rumored by the *New York Times* in April to be the product of some Republican governors who are in negotiations with the Senate over the nature of its legislative proposals. President Clinton criticizes the Republican measure as "weak on work" because it is inadequate to provide the child care, job training, and other programs needed to move recipients from welfare to work, despite setting strict work requirements. The Congressional Budget Office had previously estimated that all 50 states would fail to meet one set of job requirements under the bill.

In late May, the Senate Finance Committee approves a Republican welfare reform proposal drafted by its chair, Senator Bob Packwood of Oregon. The proposal would block grant welfare funds and eliminate all requirements for states to spend their own money as a condition of receiving federal funds. It would also freeze spending at fiscal year 1994 levels for the next five years. Packwood states, "This bill marks a revolutionary turn in the national dialogue on welfare reform." Both the United States Conference of Mayors and the National Association of Counties oppose the measure.

The Senate Finance Committee also votes to change the Supplemental Security Income program by increasing the eligibility requirements for the program. Advocates say 160,000 children will lose benefits under the changes.

Senate Democratic leader and welfare expert Daniel Moynihan introduces his proposal for maintaining the entitlement to welfare. He describes the bill, which has no cosponsors, as more a statement of principle than an effort to have an influence on the outcome of legislation. Says Moynihan, "It is beyond belief that in the middle of the Great Depression in the 1930s, we provided for children a minimum benefit to keep them alive, and in the middle of a successful 1990s, with a $7 trillion economy, we're going to take that away."

The House of Representatives takes up a Republican measure that would ensure that the federal budget is balanced in seven years. The plan would wipe out the federal deficit, reducing future spending on government programs and creating a greater reliance on state programs.

A federal district judge in New Jersey upholds the state's controversial provision that denies increased welfare payments to mothers who have more children when they are already receiving public assistance. The law took effect in October 1992. It was alleged to interfere with a woman's reproductive rights by those who brought the suit—the National Organization for Women, Legal Services of New Jersey, and the American Civil Liberties Union.

The National Academy of Sciences issues a report recommending changes in the way poverty is measured and defined. The official definition of poverty used by the federal government is 30 years old and based on cash income before taxes. The report says the federal government should adopt a concept of poverty based on disposable income, or the amount a family has left after essential expenses and taxes. This would include noncash benefits. The report was prepared by the Panel on Poverty and Family Assistance convened in 1992.

Senate Democrats release their welfare proposal called "Work First," a counterproposal to the Republican plans that have been debated for several months. The Democratic plan would retain an entitlement to cash assistance but limit benefits to five years. The proposal also calls for recipients to sign work contracts in exchange for benefits. The plan wins immediate support from the White House.

Following increasing disagreement among legislators over how funding should be allocated, conservative analyst Robert Rector of the Heritage Foundation states in the *New York Times*: "I think the real issue in welfare reform is saving the marriage and saving the family and thereby saving society. So I'm a little distressed when the debate shifts off to how to divvy up the spoils of the welfare system."

President Clinton addresses the National Governors' Association special meeting on children, held in Baltimore. He states: "Don't kid yourself. . . . Welfare reform has stopped being welfare reform primarily. Primarily, welfare reform is a way to cut spending on the poor so we don't have to worry about it and we can balance the budget in seven years and give a big tax cut largely benefiting upper-income people. That's what this is about. . . . And I just believe that we cannot allow welfare reform to be a race to the bottom."

President Clinton orders federal welfare rules altered to prevent welfare recipients who refuse to work from getting an increase in their food stamp allotments. He also announces that he will require faster federal approval of selected state welfare reform experiments, or waivers.

The Manpower Demonstration Research Corporation (MDRC), which evaluates welfare experiments, releases a report showing that strong welfare-to-work programs designed to find immediate employment for welfare recipients can lower the costs of public assistance programs by as much as 22 percent. The MDRC's report, which examines Grand Rapids, Michigan; Atlanta, Georgia; and Riverside, California, focuses on the JOBS program, which was created under the 1988 Family Support Act.

Conservative Republican Senator Phil Gramm (R-TX), who is also a Republican presidential candidate, announces a tough welfare reform proposal that would turn over control of nine major programs to the states; require 75 percent of all able-bodied welfare recipients to work; and cut off benefits to children born to families already receiving assistance, to teenage mothers, and to mothers who fail to establish their children's paternity.

1995
*cont.*

Senate Majority Leader Robert Dole introduces his own welfare reform legislation, announcing that it has the support of all 30 Republican governors. The bill would, among other things, end the long-standing federal guarantee of cash assistance for poor families with children and require state governments to move half of their adult welfare recipients into jobs by 2000. It would deny aid to unmarried teen mothers as well as additional aid for children born to a mother already receiving benefits. The bill is criticized by conservatives as not going far enough to change welfare programs, but some critics argue that further measures to reduce out-of-wedlock births will result in increased abortion rates in the states.

The Fair Share Network runs a full-page advertisement in the West Coast edition of the *New York Times* with the headline "SAVE THIS PREDICTION . . . If Congressional Extremists Win on Welfare: California Kids Will Be Begging on the Streets by the Year 2000." The Fair Share Network is a statewide coalition of California human service providers, welfare recipients, and others concerned with welfare reform at the state and national levels.

The Senate begins debate on measures to shift control of the nation's welfare system from the federal government to the states. Senate Finance Committee Chairman Robert Packwood (R-OR) states, "Welfare started as a substitute for a deceased breadwinner. But it became a lifetime support system for someone who never had a breadwinner."

The Women's Committee of One Hundred runs a full-page ad in the *New York Times* entitled "Why Every Woman in America Should Beware of Welfare Cuts. A War against Poor Women Is a War against All Women." The ad is sponsored by the National Health and Human Service Employees Union, the National Association of Social Workers, the Coalition of Labor Union Women, Catholics for a Free Choice, the Ms. Foundation for Women, and other women's and union organizations.

Senator Robert Dole (R-KS) announces that he will postpone Senate action on welfare until after the Labor Day recess in order to continue negotiations with conservative Republicans who do not think the current measure goes far enough to change the welfare system.

The Senate votes almost completely along party lines (56–41) to reject legislation by Senator Daniel Moynihan (D-NY), that would preserve the entitlement to welfare, while increasing education, training, and work rolls. Moynihan warns his Senate colleagues of the possible consequences of radical change: "We were going to empty out our mental hospitals and treat them in the community. Well, we emptied out our mental hospitals and didn't build the community centers, and the problem of homelessness began to appear. . . . If, in 10 years time, we find children sleeping on grates, picked up in the morning frozen, and ask, Why are they here, scavenging, awful to themselves, awful to one another, will anyone remember how it began? It will have begun on the House floor this spring and the Senate chamber this autumn."

Senator Majority Leader Robert Dole compromises with Republican moderates on the issue of child care for single mothers as he works to win more votes for GOP proposals that would turn welfare programs over to the states.

The Department of Health and Human Services (HHS) announces a new policy for rapid approval of certain AFDC waivers pursuant to section 1115 (a) of the Social Security Act. According to the announcement, HHS will approve waiver requests within 30 days for projects that address work requirements involving subsidized or unsubsidized jobs, community service, and rigorous job search or preparation.

The Senate passes a welfare reform compromise bill by a vote of 87–12. The bill represents a fusion of provisions championed by Dole, who states: "My view is that we made major change in welfare. It was historic. It was revolutionary."

In an October letter to congressional leaders, Alice Rivlin, director of the Office of Management and Budget,

1995
*cont.*

describes the administration's positions on key items in pending welfare reform legislation. She says the administration is "pleased that Congress finally may be within striking distance of passing comprehensive welfare reform." Rivlin also says: "In our view, the Senate bill, while far from perfect, reflects the bipartisan common ground that welfare reform must be tough on work and fair to children. The Administration will welcome a bipartisan bill that honors these common values. But a welfare reform bill that, like the House bill, is weak on work and tough on children will be unacceptable."

The Census Bureau reports that the number of poor Americans declined for the first time since 1989. The number of Americans living in poverty dropped by 1.2 million in 1994.

The *New York Times* reports that a Department of Health and Human Services draft analysis of the effect of the Senate welfare reform bill, recently backed by President Clinton, was held back from release even though it indicated that the Senate bill would push more than 1 million additional children into poverty. Democratic Senator and welfare expert Daniel Moynihan accuses the White House of suppressing the study, saying, "Those involved will take this disgrace to their graves."

Visiting the United States, Pope John Paul II asks in a speech, "Is present-day America becoming less sensitive, less caring toward the poor, the weak, the stranger, the needy? It must not!"

Congress, in its Omnibus Budget Reconciliation bill, replaces the Medicaid program with a block grant with no individual entitlement and extensive state flexibility. The new program will cut federal Medicaid spending by $163 billion below current projected spending over the next seven years. Each state will lose 18 percent of its federal funds over the next seven years relative to current law.

In early December, President Clinton vetoes the Republican plan to balance the federal budget in seven years.

Clinton denounces the plan as wrongheaded and extreme. He signs the veto with the same pen used by President Lyndon B. Johnson in 1965 to sign the Social Security Act amendments that created the Medicaid and Medicare programs. Clinton states that both of these programs would be hurt by the Republican plan, which was a key feature of the Contract with America platform on which new Republican members ran for election in November 1994.

Just before Christmas, as the House and Senate prepare to vote on the stand-alone welfare measure, Clinton states: "I am disappointed that Republicans are trying to use the words, "welfare reform" as cover to advance a budget plan that is at odds with America's values. Americans know that welfare reform is not about playing budget politics—it is about moving people from welfare to work. . . . I am determined to work with Congress to achieve real, bipartisan welfare reform. But if Congress sends me this conference report, I will veto it and insist that they try again . . .

1996    In January, on the last day of the time allowed him, President Clinton vetoes the Republican plan to overhaul the nation's primary welfare programs and end the federal guarantee of aid to the poor. He states that the Republican bill "does too little to move people from welfare to work," but said he is willing to work with Congress on a new version "to enact real, bipartisan reform." Clinton says he wants a welfare reform plan that is motivated by the urgency of reform rather than by a "budget plan that is contrary to America's values."

On 31 July, the House of Representatives passes a major welfare reform bill and sends it to the Senate. The House votes 328 to 101 for the bill, the Personal Responsibility and Work Opportunity Reconciliation Act of 1996 (H.R. 3734).

On 1 August, the U.S. Senate passes the welfare reform bill by a vote of 78 to 21. Twenty-five Democrats and all Republican senators vote for the bill. President Clinton announces that he will sign the welfare reform bill just

1996
*cont.*

passed by Congress. The bill will cut $56 billion in federal spending and give new power to the states to assist the poor. Clinton states that although the bill "has serious flaws, this is the best chance we will have for a long time to complete the work of ending welfare as we know it."

On 22 August, President Clinton signs the new law that reverses decades of federal policy; it ends the guarantee of cash assistance to the poor. The law reduces federal spending for the poor and requires the states to take a new role in assisting the poor through employment.

# Biographical Sketches 3

This chapter contains brief biographical sketches of some key figures in the debate about welfare reform. Relatively few people have become well-known because of the debate. Numerous researchers and policymakers have played crucial roles in the background. Those whose names have become public have most often been those in political life; there are no famous people on welfare who are at the center of the debate. While the federal program that is discussed the most is Aid to Families with Dependent Children (AFDC), a program that primarily serves poor mothers with children, there are relatively few women who have been prominent in this important issue.

## Mary Jo Bane

Mary Jo Bane was appointed assistant secretary for children and families at the U.S. Department of Health and Human Services (HHS) in the Clinton Administration. This position gave her the responsibility to oversee more than 60 federal assistance programs, including Aid to Families with Dependent Children (AFDC) and Head Start. She co-chaired President Clinton's Working Group on Welfare Reform, Family Support, and Independence. She brought to her role her experience as both a political appointee at the state level and as an academic in public policy. She was previously the commissioner of the New York State Department of Social Services and held several faculty positions at the Kennedy School of Government and the School of Education at Harvard University. Bane was a long-time colleague of David Ellwood. She resigned her position in HHS in protest against the new welfare law in September 1996.

## Bill Clinton

Bill Clinton was elected as a Democratic president who pledged to "end welfare as we know it," during the 1992 campaign. He brought to the White House his experience as governor of Arkansas, where he developed a welfare reform program himself. Because of his experience as governor, he sought to be responsive to states' desires for flexibility in administering their programs and acting ahead of federal reform. He instituted waiver actions at the federal level that permitted many states to undertake experimental programs even while congressional debate on welfare was unresolved. Many liberals were afraid that Clinton would allow a welfare reform bill to become law that was too harsh in its approach, just so that he could keep his campaign pledge. However, after much public pressure, he vetoed the Republican supported welfare reform legislation that came before him in January 1996. He cited the need for legislation that carried expectations of work and responsibility for parents but was not hard on children. He supported time-limited benefits and work requirements, as well as increased child support measures. President Clinton signed welfare reform legislation in August 1996 (see Chapter 5).

## Robert Dole

Robert Dole was the Republican Senate Majority Leader and longtime Republican Senator from Kansas until his resignation in 1996 to run for president from the Republican party. He was elected to the Senate in 1969 as a moderate Republican. He served 8 years in the House of Representatives before being elected to the Senate. He ran for his party's nomination for president several times since 1980 and was President Gerald Ford's running mate for Vice President. Dole had previously run for president of the United States and campaigned for his party's nomination in the

1996 primaries. Despite his history in the Republican party, he backed civil rights legislation in previous administrations. He was a staunch defender of President Richard Nixon who proposed an unsuccessful welfare reform plan. Dole had a record as a hero in World War II and had been a local public official in Kansas before entering national politics. In his role in Kansas, he had the responsibility of administering assistance programs, and he recounted in speeches his own experience of signing assistance checks for his own family during hard times. During the welfare reform debate, he did not take the more extreme positions of some of his Republican counterparts in the House of Representatives. He emphasized the importance of work, but he also endorsed the basic notion of persons in need being able to receive help on a temporary basis.

## Marian Wright Edelman

Marian Wright Edelman has been best known as founder and president of the Children's Defense Fund, a major national child advocacy organization. Her organization focused its efforts on the needs of children, thus avoiding the often contentious debate about issues and needs of poor parents. She was sharply critical of federal welfare reform legislation and urged President Clinton publicly to veto it because of its impact on children. President Clinton's wife, Hillary, was formerly involved with the Children's Defense Fund and well-known as a children's advocate. Edelman called for a massive march for children in early 1996, as a means of demonstrating the non-partisan nature of the needs of the nation's children. Edelman began her career as a civil rights lawyer and was the first black woman admitted to the Mississippi bar. She founded the Children's Defense Fund in 1973. She is the author of *The Measure of Our Success* (1992).

## David Ellwood

David Ellwood first became involved in the welfare reform debate from his position as professor of public policy at the John F. Kennedy School of Government at Harvard University. Ellwood was a colleague of Mary Jo Bane. He was formerly assistant secretary of health and human services in the Clinton Administration, where he was deeply involved in the welfare reform debate. He subsequently returned to Harvard to resume his position. Ellwood wrote the book *Poor Support* in 1988 which proposed changes in the AFDC program to time limit benefits and assist recipients with training, tax credits, health benefits, child care, and jobs.

## John Engler

John Engler is the Republican governor of Michigan, which eliminated its General Assistance program for adults in 1991. He is viewed as one of two key Republican governors on welfare issues, because of his early efforts to reform welfare, including the General Assistance program. His ending of the General Assistance program resulted in more than 80,000 persons losing their benefits; some of them built a shantytown in front of the state capitol. Engler's approval rating dropped below 30 percent of the voters. However, he recovered politically and was reelected in 1994 with more than 61 percent of the vote—the biggest victory margin for a Republican governor since 1928 and the second biggest plurality in Michigan history. He has since been regarded by other Republicans as a model for their own reform efforts, both in the states and at the federal level. He was deeply involved in the Congressional welfare debate.

## Newt Gingrich

Newt Gingrich became Speaker of the U.S. House of Representatives after the 1994 elections put the Republican party in the majority. Gingrich, a Republican representative from Georgia, was first elected to the House in 1978. Gingrich became a proponent of "dynamic conservatism"; he was elected Republican minority whip in the House of Representatives in 1989. He believes in a smaller federal government as well as government playing a role in supporting traditional morals. He became Speaker after the election of a Republican majority whose new members endorsed the legislative agenda outlined in the Contract with America. Gingrich supported the end of an entitlement to welfare, emphasis on marriage and ending out-of-wedlock births, and harsh penalties for women who did not comply with program requirements.

## Lyndon Johnson

Lyndon Johnson was the Democratic president whose "Great Society" and "War on Poverty" programs of the 1960s made up the second wave of major social welfare legislation in the U.S. The legislative program proposed by Johnson concentrated on antipoverty, health, education, conservation, and urban planning measures. Legislation passed to raise social security payments. The bill also provided for hospital benefits (Medicare) for most persons 65 years of age and over. Johnson won cooperation from the 89th Congress, in which Democrats outnumbered Republicans by a ratio of more than two to one. A bill creating a Cabinet-level Department of Housing and Urban Development (HUD) was passed though similar legislation urged by other presidents had been rejected. Other major measures enacted in 1965 included an omnibus housing bill.

## Daniel Patrick Moynihan

Daniel Patrick Moynihan has long been viewed as the Congress' welfare expert and key legislative leader on welfare issues. Moynihan was raised in a middle class neighborhood in New York, worked as a stevedore, and then attended Tufts University and the London School of Economics. Moynihan was assistant secretary of labor (1963–65); assistant to the president for urban affairs (1969–71); ambassador to India (1973–75); ambassador to the United Nations (1975–76). He served as President Richard Nixon's advisor on urban affairs when he proposed a guaranteed minimum annual income for poor Americans, a plan that was defeated by both liberals and conservatives. He was also the chief proponent of the Family Support Act, passed by a vote of 96-1 and signed into law by President Ronald Reagan. He has been a senator since 1977. He has authored 16 books on poverty and welfare issues. He warned against harsh welfare reform in the Clinton Administration, because of the adverse results for poor children.

## Richard Nixon

Richard Nixon was the Republican president of the United States who proposed the Family Assistance Plan in 1969, as a radical departure from existing welfare programs. He urged the establishment of national minimum standards for welfare payments and the sharing of federal revenue with the states. He called for drastic change in the nation's welfare system through the adoption of the Family Assistance Plan, which would alter programs unchanged

since the 1930s. The Nixon plan proposed that every unemployed family of four would receive at least $1,600 a year from
the federal government. This assistance would provide the dif-
ference between low wages and what was needed to live above
the poverty line. Working poor people would be allowed to
keep more of their pay under the plan, and all able-bodied people (except mothers with small children) would be required to
work or be in a job training program. In a plan called the "new
federalism" the program would eventually be turned over to
the states. The proposal provoked immediate controversy and
ultimately failed.

## Abraham Ribicoff

Abraham Ribicoff was secretary of the U.S. Department of
Health, Education, and Welfare from 1961–62, under President
John F. Kennedy. During that period, he made the enactment of
Medicare a priority, though the program failed to pass until 1965.
He was also responsible for the revision of the 1935 Social Security Act, including the 1962 Public Welfare Amendments which
permitted federal aid to 2-parent families. Though this provision
was intended to curtail the desertion of families by their male
heads, many states continued to restrict benefits to female-
headed households. Ribicoff subsequently became a Democratic
senator from Connecticut.

## Franklin Roosevelt

Franklin Roosevelt was the Democratic president whose New
Deal social welfare programs form the basis of existing welfare
programs. The modern era of welfare programs in the United
States can be traced to the years of the Great Depression following the stock market crash of 1929, and the "New Deal" programs Roosevelt introduced as president. He brought to the
presidency his experiences as governor of New York, where he
had overhauled the public welfare law, instituted old age pensions, and developed other social programs. As a result, there
were four primary and enduring developments in the nation's
welfare system: Social Security, Aid to Dependent Children
(ADC), Workmen's Compensation, and Unemployment Insurance. The passage of the Social Security Act established federal
responsibility for public welfare. The programs were intended to

help persons who had experienced bad luck, suffered a misfortune, or could somehow be viewed as blameless for their predicament.

## Robert Rector

Robert Rector is a policy analyst for the conservative Heritage Foundation in Washington, D.C. He has been an advisor to the House Republicans on the welfare reform proposals and is highly regarded among conservative politicians and analysts in the debate. Rector's position is based on the belief that welfare recipients should work from the time they receive assistance. He views welfare reform as based on the control of out-of-wedlock births, not the ending of poverty, or the provision of job training. He believes "behavioral poverty," not "material poverty," is the problem to be solved. It was Rector's idea to put forward the controversial idea of orphanages for poor children in the debate. Rector first became involved in legislative reform issues in 1990 during the drafting of child care proposals, which became more conservative through his efforts. Rector is closely tied to other key conservative organizations, including the Christian Coalition and the Family Research Council.

## Tommy Thompson

Tommy Thompson is the Republican governor of Wisconsin, which had one of the nation's most drastic waiver plans implemented under the Bush administration. Under the "Work not Welfare" plan, referred to as a "cold turkey" plan, a strict time limit of two years of assistance was imposed in some counties. With John Engler of Michigan, he is viewed as one of two key Republican governors on welfare issues. He lobbied extensively in the Congress for the Personal Responsibility Act, and proposed for Wisconsin the replacement of cash assistance with job placement assistance. Thompson proposed tripling state spending on child care assistance and providing health insurance for parents who became employed. These two key issues of child care and health insurance have been widely viewed as the major disincentives for leaving welfare and seeking employment.

# Facts and Statistics about Welfare Programs

# 4

This chapter provides resources for understanding key areas of the welfare reform debate. The resources provided here are in the form of background information about several major welfare programs, as well as facts and figures about aspects of the welfare programs. Material in this chapter is drawn from research by issue-oriented organizations concerned with the welfare programs, as well as from government agencies. Material on specific proposals in the welfare reform debate may be found in Chapter 5.

## Poverty Level

The U.S. Department of Health and Human Services (HHS) annually publishes guidelines on the dollar figure of income for households of various sizes that will constitute the poverty-level eligibility for the coming year. They reflect changes in the Consumer Price Index (CPI) of the previous year. While this measure of poverty is not without controversy, it is used for many federal programs. Following are those figures as published in 1996. These are guidelines for all states (including the District of Columbia) except Alaska and Hawaii.

| Size of family unit | Poverty guideline |
|:---:|:---:|
| 1 | $7,740 |
| 2 | $10,360 |
| 3 | $12,980 |
| 4 | $15,600 |
| 5 | $18,220 |
| 6 | $20,840 |
| 7 | $23,460 |
| 8 | $26,080 |

# Means-Tested Programs

This and the following sections offer general information about existing welfare programs. Those covered here include income assistance (such as Aid to Families with Dependent Children [AFDC], General Assistance, and Supplemental Security Income [SSI]); medical care (Medicaid); food and nutrition assistance (food stamps, Women, Infants, and Children nutrition program [WIC], school breakfasts and lunches); housing assistance (public housing and other housing assistance); education and training (Job Training Partnership Act, Head Start); and other programs for low-income people (such as energy assistance).

The following description of means-tested programs for low-income individuals summarizes the primary characteristics of this form of aid.

Over the years, nearly 80 means-tested programs for low-income individuals and families have been created to help meet the specific needs of various groups. In fiscal year 1992, the federal government spent about $208 billion on these programs.

Means-tested programs are restricted to individuals or families whose income falls below defined levels and who meet certain other eligibility criteria established for each program. To qualify for assistance, applicants generally must show proof of income and other documentation, which administering agencies then verify.

Certain means-tested programs, called entitlements, guarantee assistance to individuals and families as long as they meet the income and eligibility tests. It is important to note that not all entitlement programs of the federal government are either explicitly means-tested or targeted to low-income people.

The largest of the targeted entitlement programs for low income persons are: Aid to Families with Dependent Children
(AFDC), Medicaid, Food Stamps, and Supplemental Security Income (SSI). Other means-tested programs, such as housing and
energy assistance programs, are non-entitlements. When programs are not entitlements, they do not guarantee assistance to
all those who qualify. Instead, they provide qualified applicants
with support within the limits of available funds.

For instance, in the case of housing assistance in the form
of public housing units and housing subsidies, it is estimated
that available assistance reaches only one in four qualified persons. The federal government has never made available the
funds or provided the entitlement to this form of assistance that
does exist in programs such as AFDC. So only a minority of
those who need and qualify for housing assistance can actually
receive it. In the case of housing assistance, this means that
there are long waiting lists for assistance.

. . . while there are about 80 means-tested programs, most
of the federal cost comes from five programs. The many means-
tested programs are costly and difficult to administer . . . [and]
sometimes overlap one another, . . . they are often so narrowly
focused that gaps in services hinder clients . . . although advanced computer technology is essential to efficiently running
the programs, it is not being effectively developed or used. Due
to their size and complexity, many of these programs are inher-
ently vulnerable to fraud, waste, and abuse. We also point out
that some of our work has shown that the welfare system is
often difficult for clients to navigate.

**Source**: "Means-Tested Programs: An Overview, Problems, and Issues."
Statement of Jane Ross, Director, Income Security Issues, Health, Education, and Human Services Division, General Accounting Office, Washington, D.C. Testimony before the Subcommittee on Department
Operations, Nutrition and Foreign Agriculture, Committee on Agriculture, House of Representatives. 7 February 1995.

# Aid to Families with Dependent Children (AFDC)

AFDC is a federal and state program that provides cash assistance to families with children under 18 years of age who are deprived of the support of one or both of their parents. AFDC was

established by the Social Security Act of 1935 as the Aid to Dependent Children (ADC) program.

An adult without children is not eligible for AFDC. Pregnant women are eligible for assistance depending on the plan of their state. Two-parent families are eligible in many states under the AFDC-Unemployed Parent (AFDC-UP) program. A state plan must be filed with the U.S. Department of Health and Human Services (HHS), the federal agency that administers AFDC and other welfare programs. In many states, AFDC recipients are required to participate in education, job training, or job-search programs. If eligible for AFDC, a family is also eligible for Medicaid and food stamps.

To be eligible for AFDC, families must have children under age 18 who are deprived of the support or care of one or both parents. A child may be considered deprived due to the death of one or both parents; existence of only one legal parent due to adoption; or continued absence of one or both parents due to desertion or abandonment, divorce, marital separation, incarceration, temporary cancellation of physical custody, deportation of a parent from the United States, or the inability of a parent to enter the United States.

States define need (standard of need), set benefit levels (payment standards), establish limits on other income and resources, and administer the AFDC program. Maximum payments vary greatly from state to state. The need standard includes, but does not necessarily adequately cover, basic consumption items such as food, clothing, shelter, utilities, and personal and household items.

## General Facts about AFDC

- From 1970 to 1993, the number of recipients increased from 7.4 million to 14.1 million, or 91 percent.

- In 1993, the average monthly enrollment was about 5.0 million; 359,000 of the recipient families were in the unemployed parent program.

- Actual expenditures for benefits increased 44 percent after inflation, from $15.5 billion in 1970 to $22.3 billion in 1993.

- After adjusting for inflation, the average monthly benefit for a family was $676 in 1970 and $373 in 1993—a reduction of 45 percent.

# AFDC Figures (Fiscal Year 1992 Data)

Information released by the Census Bureau in March 1995 showed the following:

- About 14 million people were receiving AFDC at that time, including 3.8 million mothers age 15 to 44; 500,000 mothers age 45 and over; 300,000 fathers living with dependent children; and 9.7 million children

- Nearly half of women on AFDC have never been married

- The average mother on AFDC gave birth at age 20, compared to age 23 for women not on AFDC

- The average AFDC family has 2.6 children, compared to 2.1 for families not on AFDC

- Almost half of AFDC mothers did not complete high school, compared to 15 percent of women not on AFDC

- More white women of childbearing age receive AFDC than black or Hispanic women, but black and Hispanic women receive AFDC in disproportionate numbers

- About 9 percent of foreign-born women are on AFDC, compared to slightly less than 11 percent of native-born mothers

The housing situation of AFDC recipients is as follows:

Living in own home: 4.4 percent

Living in homeless or emergency shelter: 0.1 percent

Living in public housing: 9.1 percent

Receiving Housing and Urban Development rent subsidy: 12.1 percent

Receiving other subsidy: 1.7 percent

Living in private-market housing: 63.5 percent

- Of all AFDC families, 87.3 percent participate in food stamp or donated-food programs.

The number of months the average family spends on AFDC is:

6 or less: 18.9 percent

7 to 12: 15.0 percent

13 to 18: 10.9 percent

19 to 24: 8.4 percent

25 to 36: 12.9 percent

37 to 48: 8.3 percent

49 to 60: 5.8 percent

**Source:** U.S. House Committee on Ways and Means. *Overview of Entitlement Programs ("Green Book"),* 401–402, 409, 410.

# AFDC and Other Assistance Programs

States must provide Medicaid to families who receive AFDC. States must also extend this coverage to pregnant women and children up to age six if family income is below 133 percent of poverty, and certain other persons. Most AFDC families also receive food stamps. AFDC families are also required to participate in child support enforcement efforts aimed at establishing paternity for children, signing over rights to support to the state agency, and cooperating with the state in recovering child support. Families who receive AFDC automatically qualify for the services of the state child support enforcement (CSE) agency.

The Social Security Act (Title IV-A) also permits states to choose to operate an Emergency Assistance program for families with children in need, regardless of whether those families are eligible for AFDC. Payments under the program may be used for emergency aid. Most states presently use the program, and its costs have been rising. States can also elect to include provision for covering special needs of AFDC recipients in the state standard of need. These include special diet requirements, training or educational expenses, and costs associated with pregnancy.

# The JOBS Program

The Family Support Act of 1988 (Public Law 100-485) was the last major reform of the AFDC program. It established the Job Opportunities and Basic Skills (JOBS) Training Program, which also includes supportive services. JOBS was a new employment, education, and training program for AFDC recipients. It replaced the Work Incentive Program (WIN) and other existing programs.

JOBS was an effort to ensure that AFDC families had education, training, and employment opportunities that would assist them in avoiding long-term welfare enrollment. Long-term welfare use is generally regarded as undesirable and synonymous with dependence. Since JOBS was a prior experiment with some of the same goals as more recent efforts to alter the welfare programs, it offers a useful comparison in several ways. For instance, the program was required to be well established in each state by late 1992, so some of its results are available as well as information about how the state programs were constructed. On the other hand, some policymakers think that JOBS has only just begun to operate fully and that it is still too early either to make more alterations in welfare programs or to judge the program's results and effectiveness. Information is provided in this chapter about JOBS because some research has produced helpful information about needs and gaps in the program that may be applicable to other reform efforts.

## Federal JOBS Requirements

Every state is required to have a JOBS program, operating under a plan approved by the secretary of the Department of Health and Human Services. Every state was required to implement its plan by October 1, 1990. Every state was also required to have JOBS operating in every government subdivision of the state (such as counties) by October 1, 1992. All states met the implementation date requirement. Some states complied early. By January 1994, all were operating a statewide program.

States also had minimum enrollment targets to meet under JOBS. By fiscal year 1992, for example, states had to enroll at least 11 percent of AFDC recipients who had not been otherwise exempted. About 16 percent were enrolled. States also had to expand their funding in order to use similar federal funds. Tight state budgets prevented this from happening in many states. In fiscal year 1993, only about 70 percent of federal funds were claimed by the states. Only 16 states claimed their full amount of JOBS funds from the federal government.

## JOBS Program Administration

JOBS is administered by the Department of Health and Human Services, the federal agency with jurisdiction over the AFDC program. The office of the assistant secretary for children and families is responsible for JOBS. In the states, the state welfare agency administers the program and may provide services directly or by contract with other pubic agencies or private or community-based organizations.

States must require AFDC recipients to take part in JOBS unless they are ill, incapacitated, elderly, needed in the home for someone else affected by one of these factors, in charge of a very young child, employed 30 hours a week, a minor or in school, or in the late stages of pregnancy.

The federal match portion of JOBS funding is a capped entitlement. The formula is complex and based on a number of factors. However, an exception to this formula is a separate and open-ended entitlement or child care when participating in JOBS. The availability of funded services such as child care, essential to employment and education, is one of the dividing issues for AFDC recipients and working poor people. A working person living in poverty or near it may resent the burden of finding and funding child care without government assistance, or of having no reliable child care because of the cost involved. Looking at an AFDC recipient in JOBS receiving child care assistance may raise the question of why government supports the provision of such a needed service for a person who may be only a few dollars away in income. Similarly, the transition out of AFDC to work poses the problem of time-limited transitional child care assistance. At some point, the newly employed former AFDC recipient must bear the cost of child care, as does the previously described poor working person. The potential loss of child care, or the transition to an employment income that may in fact be less than AFDC benefits after child care expenses, may not present an incentive for a JOBS participant to succeed.

JOBS also includes incentives for states to target funds to certain populations of recipients, or face a reduced match. These groups include families in which the parent is under 24 and has not completed high school or has little work experience; families in which the youngest child may soon be ineligible for benefits because of age; and families that have recently received benefits for a relatively long period of time.

Each JOBS participant must be evaluated by the state with regard to education, child care, and supportive services needed, plus the individual's skills, prior employment experience, and employability. An employment plan is developed for each individual. The state may require the person to make an agreement specifying individual requirements under the program, and the service to be offered by the state. This, in effect, is a contract with the individual.

The state may also provide a case manager, a person to work with the participant in obtaining needed services and monitoring the individual's participation and progress in the program. Almost all states provide a case manager to each individual.

## JOBS Services and Activities

Each state is required to offer a variety of services and activities for JOBS, but may also vary which of these are available in parts of the state. Required services are:

- Education programs, including high school or high school equivalency, basic and remedial education, education for people with limited English-language skills

- Job skills training

- Job-readiness training

- Job development and placement

- Supportive services

States must also offer two of the following: group and individual job search, on-the-job training, work supplementation programs, or community work-experience programs.

## JOBS Status of AFDC Caseloads

In 1995, the General Accounting Office reported that according to the U.S. Department of Health and Human Services, 57 percent of the exempt AFDC caseload and 30 percent of the nonexempt caseload was not participating in JOBS and that 2 percent of the exempt AFDC caseload and 11 percent of the nonexempt caseload was participating in JOBS.

## Priority Populations before and under JOBS

According to a 1991 General Accounting Office report, the following priority populations were identified by the states before and after the passage of the JOBS program:

26 states gave priority to job-ready people before JOBS;

18 states gave priority to these persons under JOBS.

7 states gave priority to teen parents less than 20 years of age without a high school degree or work experience before JOBS;

45 states gave priority to these people under JOBS.

4 states gave priority to young parents aged 20–24 without a high school diploma or work experience before JOBS;

41 gave priority to these people under JOBS.

17 states gave priority to long-term aid recipients who received AFDC for any 36 of the last 60 months before JOBS;

45 states gave priority to these people under JOBS.

13 states gave priority to individuals with children who in two years would be old enough to make the family ineligible for AFDC before the JOBS program;

44 states gave priority to these people under JOBS.

**Source:** U.S. General Accounting Office. *States Begin JOBS, But Fiscal and Other Problems May Impede Their Progress.* Washington, D.C.: GAO, 1991 (GAO/HRD-91-106), 26.

## States' JOBS Program Philosophies

According to a 1991 General Accounting Office report:

32 states emphasized immediate job placement before JOBS;

9 states emphasized this under JOBS.

8 states emphasized long-term education and training before JOBS;

26 states emphasized this under JOBS.

8 states emphasized the provision of services needed by individuals before JOBS;

10 states emphasized this under JOBS.

**Source:** U.S. General Accounting Office. *States Begin JOBS, But Fiscal and Other Problems May Impede Their Progress.* Washington, D.C.: GAO, 1991 (GAO/HRD-91-106), 27.

## Outcome Indicators Used by States in JOBS Programs

According to a 1995 report by the General Accounting Office, states used the following outcome indicators to evaluate performance in the JOBS program:

- Participants entering employment: 49 states

- Hourly wages at hire: 42 states

- Participants no longer receiving AFDC due to employment: 33 states

- Job-retention rate: 26 states

- Participants with reductions in AFDC due to employment: 24 states

- Education or training achievement: 24 states

**Source:** U.S. General Accounting Office. *Welfare to Work: Measuring Outcomes for JOBS Participants.* Washington, D.C.: GAO, 1995 (GAO/HEHS-95-86), 9.

## Activities of JOBS Participants

According to a 1995 report of the General Accounting Office, JOBS participants engaged in the following activities (participants may be enrolled in more than one activity):

- Postsecondary education: 121,000

- High school or GED: 85,000

- Job skills training: 80,000

- Job search: 75,000

- Job-readiness training: 70,000
- Work experience program: 59,000
- Adult basic or remedial education: 56,000
- English As a Second Language program: 19,000
- On-the-job training: 3,000
- Work supplementation: 1,000

**Source:** U.S. General Accounting Office. *Welfare to Work: Most AFDC Training Programs Not Emphasizing Job Placement.* Washington, D.C.: GAO, 1995 (GAO/HEHS-95-113), 38.

# Availability of Services

According to a General Accounting Office report in 1995, services in several categories were available to participants in local JOBS programs in early 1994: education and training, and child care, transportation, and other supportive services.

## *Education and Training Programs*
- Postsecondary education: 99 percent
- High school or GED: 100 percent of programs
- Community work experience: 97 percent
- Adult basic or remedial education: 94 percent
- Job skills training: 95 percent
- Job search: 95 percent
- Job-readiness training: 93 percent
- On-the-job training: 73 percent
- English As a Second Language program: 70 percent
- Work supplementation: 22 percent

**Source:** U.S. General Accounting Office. *Welfare to Work: Participants' Characteristics and Services Provided in JOBS.* Washington, D.C.: GAO, 1995 (GAO/HEHS-95-93), 11.

## *Supportive Services*
- Child case assistance: 100 percent

- Transportation assistance: 99 percent

- Assistance with other work-related expenses: 95 percent

- Assistance with other supportive services: 92 percent

**Source:** U.S. General Accounting Office. *Welfare to Work: Participants' Characteristics and Services Provided in JOBS.* Washington, D.C.: GAO, 1995 (GAO/HEHS-95-93), 11.

## *Availability of Child Care, Transportation, and Other Support*

According to a 1991 General Accounting Office report, 36 states indicated that the need for child care exceeds the overall supply in their state. The need for transportation is greater than the supply in 42 states. No state indicated that the availability of either child care or transportation exceeded the need in the state, although three or four states indicated that they did not know the status of the situation.

**Source:** U.S. General Accounting Office. *Welfare to Work: States Begin JOBS, But Fiscal and Other Problems May Impede Their Progress.* Washington, D.C.: GAO, 1991 (GAO/HRD-91-106), 34.

According to a 1995 General Accounting Office report, JOBS programs identified transportation problems as the reason participants did not receive the following:

- Postsecondary education: 77 percent

- High school or GED: 76 percent

- Job skills training: 81 percent

- Job search: 72 percent

- Job-readiness training: 64 percent

- Adult basic or remedial education: 74 percent

Lack of JOBS staff was cited as the reason participants did not receive the following:

- Postsecondary education: 50 percent

- High school or GED: 59 percent

- Job skills training: 57 percent

- Job search: 68 percent

- Job-readiness training: 65 percent

- Adult basic or remedial education: 59 percent

Lack of community services was cited as the reason participants did not receive the following:

- Postsecondary education: 50 percent

- High school or GED: 40 percent

- Job skills training: 75 percent

- Job search: 50 percent

- Job-readiness training: 50 percent

- Adult basic or remedial education: 45 percent

**Source:** U.S. General Accounting Office. *Welfare to Work: Participants' Characteristics and Services Provided in JOBS.* Washington, D.C.: GAO, 1995 (GAO/HEHS-95-93), 16.

## *Failings of Current Service Delivery System*

The following problems have been cited as causing frequent disruptions in the delivery of welfare-related services:

- Needed services are difficult to access. *Examples:* Clients must travel to multiple locations; clients must complete many applications and undergo multiple assessments.

- Needed services are unavailable. *Examples:* Specialized service is not available in every geographic area; available services are insufficient to meet demand.

- Services delivered lack continuity. *Examples:* Service providers fail to coordinate the planning of their services; comprehensive service plans are not developed for clients.

- Services are crisis-oriented. *Examples:* Preventive services are inadequate; clients must wait for a problem to reach the crisis level before receiving services.

- Service programs lack accountability. *Examples:* Programs receive funding based on number of clients served rather than on outcome of service provided; few providers collect data to evaluate the success of their programs.

**Source:** U.S. General Accounting Office. *Integrating Human Services.* Washington, D.C.: GAO, 1992 (GAO/HRD-92-108), 12.

## Child Care and Welfare Reform

Child care is seen by many as one of two crucial components to labor force participation for mothers on AFDC. The other is continued Medicaid health coverage for their children. While there is some federal funding for transitional child care for AFDC mothers, availability of adequate and economical child care is a problem faced by many poor and working people. In September 1994 the Subcommittee on Human Resources of the Education and Labor Committee focused on the relationship between child care and welfare reform. At the hearing, the General Accounting Office presented the findings from some of its recent research showing that:

1. Child care subsidies can dramatically affect whether low-income women work.
2. Despite significant increases in federal child care funding in recent years, only a small percentage of the need is being filled.
3. The fragmentation of the child care funding streams results in unintended gaps in services.
4. As states experience more pressure to provide child care for welfare recipients, their support for working poor families declines.

# AFDC Waivers

Section 1115 of the Social Security Act allows the secretary of the Department of Health and Human Services to waive certain requirements of the AFDC program in order to permit states to carry out experimental, pilot, or demonstration projects. As AFDC rolls have grown, particularly in the last five years, states have attempted to change the behavior of recipients by operating such programs. They have also cut AFDC benefits to achieve this goal. The Clinton administration has encouraged the use of waivers to allow state governments to change AFDC operations and to permit alterations in the program even while federal welfare reform legislation is debated. The Bush administration also acted on waivers in early 1992.

Waivers are state actions to seek the waiving of federal rules for the AFDC program, so that a state can carry out an experimental, pilot, or demonstration program that would otherwise not be consistent with federal requirements. In his 1992 State of the Union message, President George Bush urged states to "replace the assumptions of the welfare state and help reform the welfare system." Two key requirements govern the granting of waivers. First, the state's proposal must be "cost-neutral" to the federal government. Second, whatever project the state undertakes (eliminating restrictions on eligibility of two-parent families, for instance) must be carefully evaluated by the state. No waiver requests were rejected by the Bush administration after this new policy went into effect. Forty-two states submitted waiver requests after the 1992 announcement, and 37 states had waiver projects in effect in mid-1996.

An examination of the waivers sought by states reveals certain areas of overlap in waiver requests. Together they stress work, family, and personal responsibility—the themes of the 1990s debate. At least 20 states sought waivers in the following program areas:

- Removing restrictions on two-parent families receiving AFDC

- Family caps that restrict the size of the grant a family receives when an additional child is born to a mother already on AFDC

- Child care changes that extend or expand the availability of child care assistance for AFDC recipients

- Increased earnings disregards, which allow people who go to work to keep a greater portion of their earnings

- Greater penalties for violating AFDC rules for those not in compliance with JOBS requirements

- Increased program asset limits (the $1,000 asset limit has not been raised since 1981), particularly affecting poor people who tried to own a car

- Time limits or work requirements

- Increased expansion of requirements to participate in JOBS

- Medicaid changes that extend or expand Medicaid coverage for AFDC families in transition to work

- Required school attendance

In early 1996, President Bill Clinton announced that states would be required to submit annual plans for keeping teen mothers on welfare in school. Previously, states could apply for waivers to test programs of this nature. Clinton's announcement meant that all states would be free to develop such programs, but would also have to show the federal government what they were doing to meet this goal. Said Clinton, "State by state, we are building a welfare system that demands work, requires responsibility, and protects our children."

# Supplemental Security Income (SSI)

The Supplemental Security Income (SSI) program is a federally administered income assistance program that is means-tested. SSI was established by Title XVI of the Social Security Act. The 1972 amendments to the Social Security Act (P.L. 92-603) established the program, which began in 1974. SSI replaced the former program of federal grants to the states for old-age assistance, aid to the blind, and aid to the permanently disabled. SSI is viewed as an income program for those without the possibility of receiving benefits from other sources.

As of December 1993, nearly 6 million people were receiving SSI benefits, which totaled about $23.6 billion. The monthly federal benefits for individuals was $446 in 1994, up from $140 in 1974. Federal benefit rates are by law indexed to the Consumer Price Index.

In the mid-1980s, rapid growth in the number of disabled persons on the program outpaced the number of people who are elderly or blind. From 1984 to 1993, the disabled population grew at an annual rate of about 9.2 percent. (Some of the increase since 1991 resulted from the revised disability definition that took effect.) SSI law permits benefits to be paid under so-called presumptive eligibility prior to a formal determination of disability or blindness if information indicates a high probability that a person is disabled or blind and otherwise eligible. SSI also pays benefits to children who are blind or disabled. In 1985, infection with AIDS was also added as a condition of presumptive eligibility, and in 1991 HIV infection was added.

Federal SSI benefits as a percent of the poverty rate for individuals was 75 percent in 1994 and 89.5 percent for families. Twenty-six states also provide a state supplement to the federal payment. Forty states also provide a special state supplement for housing needs, daily living, and protective services for the mentally retarded, chronically ill, and the frail elderly.

The Social Security Administration uses representative payees to receive or use SSI payments on behalf of SSI recipients when necessary because of the mental or physical limitations of the recipients. Representative payees are individuals, agencies, or institutions approved by the Social Security Administration. In the last few years, some attention has been directed to the required use of representative payees for persons receiving SSI because of drug- or alcohol-related disabilities. There has been concern that lack of control over the cash received by persons with addictions leads to the use of their benefits for continued alcohol or drug use. Persons who receive SSI benefits because of a disability from drug or alcohol addiction must accept treatment as a condition of SSI eligibility, must allow their treatment to be monitored, and must have a representative payee for their benefits.

A person may receive SSI and Social Security, but not both SSI and AFDC. If a parent or child is eligible for both, the parent must choose which benefit the family will receive. Also, a parent may apply for SSI, start receiving AFDC, and then drop the AFDC benefits when SSI benefits are granted.

States have three choices for determining if SSI recipients will also receive Medicaid. One choice calls for the Social Security Administration to enter into agreements with states to cover all SSI recipients. Thirty-one states follow this plan. Another choice permits states to elect Medicaid benefits for SSI recipients, but requires the individual to complete a separate Medicaid application. Seven states use this approach. The third and most restrictive choice allows states to user stricter Medicaid eligibility requirements than they do for SSI based on certain state plan requirements. Twelve states use this option.

SSI recipients may also be eligible for food stamps. Use of the food stamp program also has consequences when a state might choose to increase SSI payments by $1. Food stamps are automatically reduced by 30 cents for each additional dollar of SSI income.

SSI eligibility is limited to qualified persons who have financial and other resources within a certain dollar limit. While the details are complex, these factors can have an important and sometimes negative result for the person or household involved. Included in the resource pool are items such as household goods, personal effects, and autos.

## SSI Facts

Adults (age 18–64) who receive SSI because of a disability:

- *Major diagnosis for disability:* Mental retardation: 23.7 percent; other mental disorders: 32.2 percent

- *Representative payees:* 30.6 percent of the adult disabled or blind on SSI had a representative payee in 1993.

- *Gender:* As of 1994, 55 percent of those receiving SSI for a disability were women; 56.4 percent of those receiving benefits for blindness were women.

- *Race:* 57.6 percent of those receiving SSI for a disability in 1994 were white; 31.2 percent were black; 7.9 percent were other races.

- *Other income:* 32.4 percent of the disabled and 36.9 percent of the blind also received Social Security as of 1993.

Adults (over age 18) who receive SSI because of age:

- *Age:* 35.9 percent of those receiving benefits due to age (age 65 or older) were 80 years old or more.

- *Gender:* 73.8 percent of those receiving benefits were women.

- *Race:* 55.4 percent of those receiving benefits were white; 22.0 percent were black; 19.4 percent were other races.

- *Other income:* 65.1 percent also received Social Security benefits; 2.1 percent had earned income.

## Changes in the SSI Population

- Numbers of those receiving benefits on the basis of age are declining

- Sharp increase over the last 20 years in the numbers of children receiving SSI

- Sharp increase in the last decade in the numbers of those nonelderly persons receiving benefits because of disability or blindness

Adults with drug or alcohol addiction:

- In 1993, 79,000 persons received SSI because of addiction.

- More than 50 percent of those receiving benefits live in California or Illinois.

- About 75 percent of recipients are male.

- About 41 percent of recipients are white; 37 percent are black.

- Most recipients are addicted to alcohol.

- The Social Security Administration only knows the treatment status of about 44 percent of SSI recipients.

# General Assistance Programs

Several reports have assessed the impact of the elimination of the General Assistance (GA) program in Michigan, two years after the cuts were made. Early reports described the characteristics of the GA population and examined work, health, housing, and welfare participation in the first year after program termination.

Key findings of the University of Michigan report cited here and based on survey data include:

1. Even though most GA recipients (76 percent) had prior work experience, only 38 percent found any formal employment in either of the two post-GA years; only one in five was employed at the time of the second interview.
2. Those who worked were typically in low-wage jobs, such as janitorial or kitchen work.
3. About 15 percent of the entire former GA population was enrolled in a disability program (either SSI or SDA, the state disability assistance program) less than two years after GA termination.

4. Significant health problems, including deteriorating health, onset of chronic illness, and lack of medical insurance were reported after GA termination.
5. Only one-third of nondisabled former recipients had access to income equivalent to (or greater than) what they had while on GA, even though the maximum GA benefit for a single person was only $160 a month.

This report does not capture homeless GA recipients because of the inability to locate those who could not provide a permanent or forwarding address.

**Source:** Danziger, Sandra, and Sherrie Kossoudji. *When Welfare Ends: Subsistence Strategies of Former GA Recipients: Final Report of the General Assistance Project.* University of Michigan School of Social Work. 1995.

# Food Stamps

The food stamp program is another key federal welfare program. It is aimed at helping low-income people buy more food and improve their diets. It is administered by the Agriculture Department, which pays for coupons or food stamps and for half the state's cost of running the program. Federal rules govern what the states can do under the food stamp program, but each state also writes its own regulations. Food stamps can be spent in food stores, convenience stores, and other establishments for food items only. Food stamps can also be received by working people who meet the income guidelines.

# Medicaid

Medicaid was enacted in 1965 in the same legislation that created Medicare. At the time, Medicaid was seen as the lesser of the programs, but it has grown dramatically. It is now the primary program providing health insurance to poor people. It is available to anyone who meets the eligibility criteria.

Medicaid was originally intended to cover welfare recipients, but has been expanded to include other children and some blind and disabled persons, pregnant women, and some residents of nursing homes. About 37 million people are covered, about 50 percent of whom are children.

States and the federal government share the expense of Medicaid. States receive federal payments based on their per capita income. In poorer areas, the federal share is larger. The federal payment can range from 50 to 80 percent of Medicaid expenses. States establish their own eligibility criteria.

Medicaid covers basic inpatient and outpatient services, doctor's services, laboratory and x-ray services, home health care, early and periodic screening, diagnosis and treatment for children under age 21, family planning, prenatal care, and rural health clinics.

Medicaid was established in 1965 as a jointly funded federal-state program providing medical assistance to qualified low-income persons. Each state designs and administers its own Medicaid program, subject to federal requirements for eligibility, services covered, and provider payments. States decide whether to cover optional services and how much to reimburse providers for a particular service. The federal government pays a portion of whatever qualifying expenditures a state Medicaid program incurs. At the federal level, the program is administered by the Heath Care Financing Administration (HCFA), a Department of Health and Human Services agency.

In recent years, Medicaid costs have escalated. In 1995, federal spending on Medicaid was estimated at $89 billion; the state share is estimated at $67 billion. Federal Medicaid spending has quadrupled in the last decade and doubled over the last five years. To control these costs, some states have sought to move most or some of their Medicaid population into a capitated managed care system. However, certain provisions of the Medicaid law—such as freedom of choice and the "75-25" beneficiary requirements—inhibit states' use of managed care. States may obtain waivers of these provisions from the HCFA under the authority of section 1115 of the Social Security Act. Section 1115 offers the HCFA the authority to waive a broad range of Medicaid requirements for state demonstration projects.

In granting a waiver, the HCFA requires the applying state to demonstrate that its proposal is budget neutral—that is, that federal expenditures for the entire demonstration project will not exceed costs projected for the existing Medicaid program. Until recently, budget neutrality was expected to be achieved in each year of the demonstration. However, the HCFA now allows increased costs in some years as long as states achieve budget neutrality for the entire demonstration. The HCFA may also require the state to implement improved quality-assurance systems, which may include data collection on enrollee medical care utilization and assessment of these data to determine the adequacy of enrollee access to and quality of medical care.

As of June 1995, ten states had HHS-approved statewide waivers, eight had applications pending, and five had inquired about submitting waiver applications. In November 1993, five months after Tennessee submitted its 1115 waiver application, the HHS approved it. On 1 January 1994, Tennessee became the first state to move its Medicaid program enrollees to a statewide demonstration project.

**Source:** U.S. General Accounting Office. *Medicaid: Tennessee's Program Broadens Coverage But Faces Uncertain Future.* Washington, D.C.: GAO, 1995 (GAO/HEHS-95-186).

# Job-Training Programs

The Job Training Partnership Act of 1982 (JTPA) provides block grants to the states for training low-income youth, adults, and dislocated workers. The Job Corps program was authorized by the Economic Opportunity Act of 1964 to provide educational and vocational services to disadvantaged young people aged 14 to 24.

# Education Programs

The Head Start program was created in 1964 to prepare preschool children for school by improving nutrition and teaching social and learning skills. The Elementary and Secondary Education Act of 1965 provided federal aid to schools serving low-income students.

## Facts about the Head Start Program, Fiscal Years 1966 to 1994

Enrollment (in millions)

1966: 733,000

1970: 477,400

1975: 349,000

1980: 376,300

1985: 452,080

1990: 548,470

1991: 583,471

1992: 621,078

1993: 713,903

1994: 750,000 (est.)

**Source:** U.S. House Committee on Ways and Means. *Overview of Entitlement Programs ("Green Book"),* 1994.

# Earned Income Tax Credit (EITC)

The Earned Income Tax Credit (EITC) is a refundable tax credit available to low-income working people with children and, beginning in 1994, to low-income, single working people. Congress established the EITC in 1975 to achieve two purposes: (1) to offset the impact of Social Security taxes on low-income workers with families and (2) to encourage low-income individuals with families to seek employment rather than receive welfare.

In tax year 1993, about 14.7 million persons claimed about $15 billion in EITC benefits. To be eligible, a person must have had earned income of less than $23,050 and had one or more qualifying children who met the age, relationship, and residency requirements for the program. The Omnibus Budget Reconciliation Act of 1993 increased the number of taxpayers eligible for the credit and the credit amount. These changes will be fully effective in 1996. The maximum qualifying income for the EITC will rise to $27,000 in 1996, with the maximum credit in 1996 being $3,370. The total fiscal cost for 1996 is expected to be nearly $25 billion.

# Speeches, Reports, and Other Documents 5

This chapter offers in-depth information drawn from letters, speeches, editorials, and policy papers about reform proposals. Some originate with elected officials and federal agencies, some are from other sources. The first section contains such materials from President Bill Clinton and members of his administration. Second are materials representing conservative viewpoints. Third are materials that represent the proposals and comments of other organizations, members of Congress, and the press. Fourth are some brief historical documents reflecting comments and proposals from the Hoover, Roosevelt, Kennedy, and Reagan administrations.

## Clinton Administration Materials

### Working Group on Welfare Reform, Family Support, and Independence

President Clinton charged this working group to develop a proposal to "end welfare as we know it." The group was chaired by Bruce Reed, deputy assistant to the president for domestic policy; David Ellwood, assistant secretary for planning and evaluation in the Department of Health and Human Services (HSS); and Mary Jo Bane, assistant secretary for the administration of children and families in the HSS. Regular members of the Working Group included appointees from the HSS, the Treasury Department, the Department of Labor, the Department of Agriculture, the Office of the Vice President, the Department of Education, the Department of Commerce, the Department of Justice, the Office of Management and Budget, the Department of Housing and Urban Development, and the Council of Economic Advisers.

The Working Group was guided by four principles underlying the president's vision for reform:

- *Make work pay.* People who work should not be poor. They should get the support they need to ensure that they can work and adequately support their families. The economic support system must provide incentives that encourage families to work and not stay on welfare.
- *Dramatically improve child support enforcement.* Both parents have a responsibility to support their children. One parent should not have to do the work of two. Only one-third of single parents currently receive any court-ordered child support. The system for identifying fathers and ensuring that their children receive the support they deserve must be strengthened.
- *Provide education, training, and other services to help people get off and stay off welfare.* People should have access to the basic education and training they need to get and hold onto a job. Existing programs encouraged by the Family Support Act of 1988 need to be expanded, improved, and better coordinated.
- *Create a time-limited transitional support system followed by work.* With the first three steps in place, assistance can be made truly transitional. Those who are healthy and able to work will be expected to move off welfare quickly, and those who cannot find jobs should be provided with work and expected to support their families.

Based on these core principles, the Working Group was to develop a detailed proposal that would not simply change the welfare system but would ultimately provide an alternative to it. In February 1994, the administration's working group considered an issue paper on welfare reform. It contained the key elements of the administration's positions. Portions are excerpted here.

# Introduction

Everyone is frustrated with the welfare system. Welfare reform is designed to give people back the dignity and opportunity that comes from work and independence. It is about reinforcing work and family and opportunity and responsibility.

The current system pays cash when people lack adequate means to provide for their families. We propose a new vision aimed at helping people regain the means of supporting themselves and at holding people responsible for themselves and their families. The proposal emphasizes that work is valued by making work pay. It indicates that people should not have children until they are able to support them. It signals that parents—both parents—have responsibilities to support their children. It gives people access to the training they need, but also expects work in return. It limits cash assistance to two years, and then requires work, preferably in the private sector, but in community service jobs if necessary. Most importantly, it requires changing the culture of welfare offices, getting them out of the check-writing business and into the training and job-placement business.

Ultimately, this plan requires changing everything about the way in which we provide support to struggling families. To achieve this vision, the plan has four main elements.

## Transitional Assistance Followed by Work

Full participation

Training, education, and employment services

Time limits

Work for those who exhaust their time limit (the WORK program)

## Making Work Pay

Health care reform

Advance payment of the Earned Income Tax Credit

Child care for the working poor

## Parental Responsibility

Child support enforcement

Efforts aimed at minor mothers, responsible family planning, and prevention

Efforts to promote two-parent families

## Reinventing Government Assistance

Coordination, simplification, and improved incentives in income support programs

A performance-based system

**Source:** *Welfare Reform Issue Paper.* Prepared for meeting of the Working Group on Welfare Reform, Family Support, and Independence. 26 February 1994.

# HHS Principles and Procedures for Federal Waivers

In the 27 September 1994 *Federal Register,* the Administration for Children and Families of the Department of Health and Human Services (ACF/HHS) published a public notice of policies and procedures that the HHS will use when considering whether to grant a waiver in the Aid to Dependent Families with Children (AFDC) program to states.
The public notice discussed three issues:

1. the principles the HHS "ordinarily will consider when deciding" whether to approve a demonstration project;
2. the kinds of "procedures HHS would expect States to employ in involving the public in the development of proposed demonstration projects . . ."; and
3. the "procedure [the HHS] Department ordinarily will follow in reviewing demonstration proposals . . . "

Further, the notice establishes that "the principles and procedures described in the notice . . . are not legally binding."
HHS stated that it will consider waiver proposals that are both consistent with its policy goals and those that "test alternatives that diverge from that policy direction." HHS will not only

consider a state's ability to implement the proposal, but also the policy implications of the demonstration project, stating that it "may disapprove or limit proposals on policy grounds or because the proposal creates potential constitutional problems or violations of civil rights laws or equal protection requirements."

HHS will grant waivers that range in scale "from reasonably small state-wide [to] multi-state" projects. The duration of the demonstration will depend on many variables, but generally the department will "approve waivers of at least sufficient duration to give new policy approaches a fair test, . . . provide reasonable time for the preparation of meaningful evaluation results, . . . [and] recognize that new approaches often involve considerable start-up time. . . ." When a waiver proves itself successful, HHS will also work with the state to help make permanent statutory changes.

HSS maintained its policy of cost neutrality, saying it "believes it should be possible to apply that principle flexibly." Cost neutrality will be considered over the life of the demonstration and "will not rule out consideration of other cost neutral arrangements proposed by States." However, states may be required to conform to national welfare reform legislation. All of the waivers will be required to include an evaluation process. "Within-site randomized design is the preferred approach for most AFDC waivers."

HHS is interested in making the waiver process easier to maneuver by expanding the preapplication period, setting a well-defined schedule, providing technical assistance to states, sharing the "terms and conditions" with states before making a final decision, and other changes. In order to enable the public to have a chance to voice its opinion, the department will require states to provide a written description of the process they use for allowing public input into the waiver process. The notice also established that an announcement of new and pending waiver proposals would appear monthly in the *Federal Register* and that a 30-day period would be maintained during which HHS will accept public comment on a submitted waiver.

*Source:* U.S. Department of Health and Human Services.

# Remarks by President Bill Clinton to the National Governors' Association

. . . I want to help people on welfare, but I also want to reward people who, on their own, are off of welfare, on modest incomes, which is why we have dramatically expanded the earned income tax credit, the program that President Reagan said was the most pro-family, pro-work initiative undertaken by the United States in the last generation. Now, this year, families with children with incomes of under $28,000 will pay about $1,300 less in income tax than they would have if the laws hadn't been changed in 1993.

We also tried to change the way the government works. It's smaller than it used to be. . . . We have also tried to solve problems that have been ignored. . . . But still, the median income is about where it was two-and-a-half years ago, which means most wage-earning Americans are still working harder for the same or lower wages. And the level of anxiety is quite high.

On the social front you see the same things. The number of people on food stamps is down. The number of people on welfare is down. The divorce rate is down. . . . So what we have is a sense in America that we're kind of drifting apart. And this future that I visualize, that I think all of you share, is being rapidly embraced by tens of millions of Americans, and achieved with stunning success. But we are still being held back in fulfilling our real destiny as a country because so many people are kind of shut off from that American Dream.

I am convinced that the American people want us to go forward together. . . . Not so very long ago there were liberals who opposed requiring all people on welfare to go to work. But now almost nobody does. . . . Not so long ago there were conservatives who thought the government shouldn't spend money on child care to give welfare mothers a chance to go to work. But now nearly everybody recognizes that the single most significant failure of the Welfare Reform Act of '88 . . . was that when we decided we couldn't fund it all, we should have put more money into child care even if it meant less money in job training, because there were states that had programs for that; and that you can't expect someone to leave their children and go to work if they have to worry about the safety of the children, or if they'll actually fall behind economically for doing it because they don't have child care. We now have a broad consensus on that.

. . . If everybody who could pay their child support and who is under an order to do it, did it, we could lift 800,000 people off the welfare rolls tomorrow. That is still our greatest short-term opportunity, and we all need to do what we can to seize it.

In the State of the Union this year I asked the new Congress to join me in passing a welfare reform bill. It still hasn't

passed, because, unfortunately, in 1995 there have been ideolog-
ical and political in-fights that have stalled progress on welfare
reform and have prevented the majority, particularly in the Senate, from taking a position on it.

Some of the people on the extreme right wing of the Republican majority have held this issue hostage because they
want to force the states to implement requirements that would
deny benefits to young unmarried mothers and their children.
But I believe it's better to require young people to stay at home,
stay in school, and turn their lives around, because the objective
is to make good workers, good parents, good citizens, and successful children. That's what we're all trying to do.

So I'm against giving the states more mandates and less
money, whether the mandates come from the right or the left.
I'm also opposed to the efforts in Congress now to cut child
care because, I say again, the biggest mistake we made in the
Welfare Reform Act of '88 was not doing more in child care. We
would have had far greater success if we had invested more
money in child care than for people on welfare.

Already in the last two-and-a-half years, our administration has approved waivers for 29 states to reform welfare your
way. The first experiment we approved was for Governor Dean
to make it clear that welfare in Vermont would become a second chance, not a way of life. Governor Thompson's aggressive
efforts in Wisconsin, which have been widely noted, send the
same strong message.

Now, we can and we should do more, and we shouldn't
just wait around for the congressional process to work its way
through. We can do more based on what states already know
will work to promote work and to protect children. Therefore,
today, I am directing the Secretary of Health and Human Services to approve reforms for any state on a fast track that incor-
porates one or more of the following five strategies.

First, requiring people on welfare to work, and providing
adequate child care to permit them to do it. . . . Second, limiting
welfare to a set number of years, and cutting people off if they
turn down jobs. . . . Third, requiring fathers to pay child support or go to work to pay off what they owe. . . . Fourth, requiring under-age mothers to live at home and stay in school. Teen
motherhood should not lead to premature independence unless
the home is a destructive and dangerous environment. The
baby should not bring the right and the money to leave school,
stop working, set up a new household and lengthen the period

of dependence, instead of shortening it. . . . And finally, permitting states to pay the cash value of welfare and food stamps to private employers as wage subsidies when they hire people to leave welfare and go to work. . . .

So I say to you today, if you pass laws like these or come up with plans like these that require people on welfare to work, that cut off benefits after a certain time for those who won't work, that make teen mothers stay at home and stay in school, that make parents pay child support or go to work to earn the money to do so, or that use welfare benefits as a wage supplement for private employers who give jobs to people on welfare—if you do that, you sign them, you send them to me and we will approve them within 30 days. Then we will have real welfare reform even as Congress considers it.

Congress still does need to pass national legislation. Why? Because I don't think you ought to have to file for permission every time you do something that we already know has worked and that other states are doing. Because we do need national child support standards, time limits, work requirements and protections for children. And we do need more national support for child care.

I hope these efforts that I'm announcing today will spur the Congress to act. But we don't have to wait for them, and we shouldn't. We can do much more. If every state did the five things that I mentioned here today—every state—we would change welfare fundamentally and for the better. And we ought to begin it, and we shouldn't wait for Congress to pass a law.

There is common ground on welfare. We want something that's good for children, that's good for the welfare recipients, that's good for the taxpayers and that's good for America. . . .

**Source:** White House, Office of the Press Secretary, 31 July 1995.

# Clinton Veto of GOP Welfare Plan

On 10 January 1996, President Bill Clinton vetoed the Republican plan to overhaul the nation's primary welfare programs and end the federal guarantee of aid to the poor. Following are excerpts from the text of his official veto message.

I am returning herewith without my approval H.R. 4, the "Personal Responsibility and Work Opportunity Act of 1995." In disapproving H.R. 4, I am nevertheless determined to keep working with the Congress to enact real, bipartisan welfare reform. The current welfare system is broken and must be replaced, for the sake of the taxpayers who pay for it and the people who are trapped by it. But H.R. 4 does too little to move people from welfare to work. It is burdened with deep budget cuts and structural changes that fall short of real reform. I urge the Congress to work with me in good faith to produce a bipartisan welfare reform agreement that is tough on work and responsibility, but not tough on children and on parents who are responsible and who want to work.

I strongly support time limits, work requirements, the toughest possible child support enforcement, and requiring minor mothers to live at home as a condition of assistance, and I am pleased that these central elements of my approach have been addressed in H.R. 4.

We remain ready at any moment to sit down in good faith with Republicans and Democrats in the Congress to work out an acceptable welfare reform plan that is motivated by the urgency of reform rather than by a budget plan that is contrary to America's values. There is a bipartisan consensus around the country on the fundamental elements of real welfare reform, and it would be a tragedy for this Congress to squander this historic opportunity to achieve it. . . .

We must demand responsibility from young mothers and young fathers, not penalize children for their parents' mistakes.

I am deeply committed to working with the Congress to reach bipartisan agreement on an acceptable welfare reform bill that addresses these and other concerns. We owe it to the people who sent us here not to let this opportunity slip away by doing the wrong thing or failing to act at all.

WILLIAM J. CLINTON
THE WHITE HOUSE,
9 January 1996.

**Source:** White House.

# President Clinton Signs Welfare Reform Legislation

Following is President Clinton's early August 1996 press statement announcing his plans to sign the welfare reform measure that passed Congress.

When I ran for President four years ago, I pledged to end welfare as we know it. I have worked very hard for four years to do just that. Today, the Congress will vote on legislation that gives us a chance to live up to that promise—to transform a broken system that traps too many people in a cycle of dependence to one that emphasizes work and independence; to give people on welfare a chance to draw a paycheck, not a welfare check.

It gives us a better chance to give those on welfare what we want for all families in America, the opportunity to succeed at home and at work. For those reasons I will sign it into law. The legislation is, however, far from perfect. There are parts of it that are wrong, and I will address those parts in a moment.

But, on balance, this bill is a real step forward for our country, our values and for people who are on welfare. For 15 years I have worked on this problem, as governor and as a President. I've spent time in welfare offices, I have talked to mothers on welfare who desperately want the chance to work and support their families independently. A long time ago I concluded that the current welfare system undermines the basic values of work, responsibility and family, trapping generation after generation in dependency and hurting the very people it was designed to help.

Today we have an historic opportunity to make welfare what it was meant to be—a second chance, not a way of life. And even though the bill has serious flaws that are unrelated to welfare reform, I believe we have a duty to seize the opportunity it gives us to end welfare as we know it. Over the past three and a half years I have done everything in my power as President to promote work and responsibility, working with 41 states to give them 69 welfare reform experiments. We have also required teen mothers to stay in school, required federal employees to pay their child support, cracked down on people who owe child support and crossed state lines.

As a result, child support collections are up 40 percent, to $11 billion, and there are 1.3 million fewer people on welfare today than there were when I took office. From the outset, however, I have also worked with members of both parties in Congress to achieve a national welfare reform bill that will make work and responsibility the law of the land. I made my principles for real welfare reform very clear from the beginning. First and foremost, it should be about moving people from welfare to work. It should impose time limits on welfare. It should give

people the child care and the health care they need to move
from welfare to work without hurting their children. It should
crack down on child support enforcement and it should protect
our children.

This legislation meets these principles. It gives us a chance
we haven't had before—to break the cycle of dependency that
has existed for millions and millions of our fellow citizens, exil-
ing them from the world of work that gives structure, meaning,
and dignity to most of our lives.

We've come a long way in this debate. It's important to remember that not so very long ago, at the beginning of this very
Congress, some wanted to put poor children in orphanages and
take away all help for mothers simply because they were poor,
young and unmarried. Last year the Republican majority in
Congress sent me legislation that had its priorities backward. It
was soft on work and tough on children. It failed to provide
child care and health care. It imposed deep and unacceptable
cuts in school lunches, child welfare and help for disabled children. The bill came to me twice and I vetoed it twice.

The bipartisan legislation before the Congress today is significantly better than the bills I vetoed. Many of the worst elements I objected to are out of it. And many of the improvements I asked for are included. First, the new bill is strong on
work. It provides $4 billion more for child care so that mothers
can move from welfare to work, and protects their children by
maintaining health and safety standards for day care. These
things are very important. You cannot ask somebody on welfare
to go to work if they're going to neglect their children in doing
it.

It gives states powerful performance incentives to place
people in jobs. It requires states to hold up their end of the bar-
gain by maintaining their own spending on welfare. And it
gives states the capacity to create jobs by taking money now
used for welfare checks and giving it to employers as income
subsidies as an incentive to hire people, or being used to create
community service jobs.

Second, this new bill is better for children than the two I vetoed. It keeps the national nutritional safety net intact by eliminating the food stamp cap and the optional block grant. It drops
the deep cuts and devastating changes in school lunch, child
welfare and help for disabled children. It allows states to use
federal money to provide vouchers for children whose parents
can't find work after the time limits expire. And it preserves the

national guarantee of health care for poor children, the disabled, pregnant women, the elderly and people on welfare.

Just as important, this bill continues to include the child support enforcement measures I proposed two years ago, the most sweeping crackdown on deadbeat parents in history. If every parent paid the child support they should, we could move 800,000 women and children off welfare immediately. With this bill we say to parents, if you don't pay the child support you owe, we will garnish your wages, take away your drivers license, track you across state lines and, as necessary, make you work off what you owe. It is a very important advance that could only be achieved in legislation. I did not have the executive authority to do this without a bill.

So I will sign this bill. First and foremost because the current system is broken. Second, because Congress has made many of the changes I sought. And, third, because even though serious problems remain in the non-welfare reform provisions of the bill, this is the best chance we will have for a long, long time to complete the work of ending welfare as we know it by moving people from welfare to work, demanding responsibility and doing better by children . . .

**Source:** Press Release, 31 July 1996, Office of the Press Secretary, White House.

# Conservative Viewpoints

## The Contract with the American Family

The Christian Coalition is one of the interest organizations actively involved in the welfare reform debate. The following excerpts are from a coalition proposal on family issues.

. . . The Contract with the American Family is a bold agenda for Congress intended to strengthen families and restore common-sense values. The Contract represents a valuable contribution to a congressional agenda beyond the first hundred days. These provisions are the ten suggestions, not the Ten Commandments. There is no deadline or specified time period during which they are to be enacted. But Congress would be well advised to act with all due and deliberate speed. The provisions in the Contract enjoy support from 60 to 90 percent of the American people.

These items do not represent the pro-family movement's entire agenda. There are many other prominent pro-family organizations that will work on many other issues—women in combat, welfare reform, budget policy—in the months ahead. This contract is designed to be the first word, not the last word, in developing a bold and incremental start to strengthening the family and restoring values.

**Source:** Christian Coalition, Washington, D.C.

## Remarks by Former Senate Majority Leader Robert Dole

At the same July 1995 meeting of the National Governors' Association addressed by President Bill Clinton, then–Senate Majority Leader Bob Dole (R-KS) discussed reforming the nation's welfare system. His remarks are excerpted below. Dole discussed the direction of the Senate Republican leadership proposal. He spoke about three main principles that his leadership bill would follow. Dole resigned his post in mid-1996 to run for president.

I think first, the first principle that ought to strike home is that welfare reform should be designed and run by those closest to the problem, the states. . . . The answer is not more waivers. Governors should not have to play a game of "Mother may I." The waiver process only perpetuates a flawed system. . . .

Our second principle is that real welfare reform must include a real work requirement, which in no uncertain terms requires able-bodied welfare recipients to find a job, not stay at home, and not stay in a training program forever, but to go to work in a job, hopefully in a real job in the private sector. . . .

Then our final principle is that no program with an unlimited budget will ever be made to work effectively and efficiently; therefore, we must put a cap on welfare spending. . . .

**Source:** Office of Senator Robert Dole.

## Robert Rector on Welfare Reform

Robert Rector is a policy analyst for the conservative Heritage Foundation in Washington, D.C. He has been an adviser to the House Republicans on welfare reform proposals and is highly regarded among conservative politicians and analysts in the debate. Rector's position is based on the belief that welfare recipients should work from the time they receive assistance. He views welfare reform as based on the control of out-of-wedlock births, not the ending of poverty or the provision of job training. He believes "behavioral poverty," not "material poverty," is the problem to be solved.

Rector's recommendations for reducing welfare dependency and reforming AFDC are these:

Welfare dependence can be reduced by six means: reducing illegitimacy; reducing divorce; increasing marriage among women who have had children out of wedlock but have not yet enrolled in welfare; encouraging single mothers to take jobs before they enter AFDC; increasing marriage among welfare mothers; and having welfare mothers obtain jobs . . .

. . . The Contract with America advanced three principles of welfare reform: promoting marriage and reducing illegitimacy, requiring work, and increasing state flexibility. The [National Governors' Association] plan abandons the first two of these principles despite the fact that they are supported overwhelmingly by the public. Real welfare reform must carry out the principles of the Contract.

Restoring a sensible debate on marriage and illegitimacy is crucial. This issue has been trivialized or ignored by those pretending it is merely a question of whether the family cap provision . . . should be retained or eliminated. In reality, conservatives have proposed nearly a dozen national measures aimed at reducing illegitimacy. Many were included in the Contract with America. But in each case, they have been resisted by the Washington establishment and, one by one, they have been whittled away. What is now required is a complete reorientation of the debate back to the topic of illegitimacy, and the establishment of multiple measures to deal with the problem . . .

**Source:** Heritage Foundation. *Backgrounder*: 1075. 18 March 1996.

## Speech by California Governor Pete Wilson

California Republican Governor Pete Wilson spoke at the Heritage Foundation on 6 September 1995. His speech was sponsored by the Heritage Foundation's Governors' Forum. The following comments concern Supplemental Security Income benefits paid to people with drug- or alcohol-related disabilities.

[Senate liberals have extended] federal disability benefits to individuals whose only disability is self-inflicted drug and alcohol abuse. Today, nearly 100,000 individuals collect such benefits. And the number grew nearly six-fold in five years. . . .

What alcoholic would pass up a chance to have the taxpayers pick up their bar tab? That's why the House welfare bill ended this absurd practice next month. . . . That's not only an insult to taxpayers, it's an outrage for the federal government to be subsidizing someone's addiction. As the head of one homeless shelter described it, it's "suicide on the installment plan." It's wrong and it's got to stop. . . .

## Remarks of Michigan Governor John Engler

John Engler is the Republican governor of Michigan, which eliminated its General Assistance (GA) program for adults in 1991. He is viewed as one of two key Republican governors on welfare issues because of his early efforts to reform welfare, including the GA program. He was deeply involved in the congressional welfare debate. Following are excerpts from remarks made by Engler to the conservative Cato Institute in Washington, D.C., in March 1995.

. . . I've already mentioned my decision to abolish GA to over 80,000 able-bodied adults without children. For those with children and on AFDC, I said: You are going to sign a Social Contract; you must go to work. To make sure work paid, we removed every barrier we could that was preventing recipients from going to work.

Unfortunately, to remove barriers, the governors have had to go to Washington, hat in hand, and practically beg the feds to let us fix a broken system. Recipients faced limits on how many hours they could work a week, how much they could earn a week, how much they could save—these are still federal law. But because of waivers we swept away all that and said: Go to work. And today, Michigan has one of the best welfare-to-work track records in the nation. In the last two years, we closed over 55,000 cases and saved taxpayers over $100 million.

**Source:** Cato Institute, Washington, D.C.

# Testimony of William J. Bennett

William J. Bennett is a conservative Republican and former drug czar and secretary of education in past administrations. He has been a frequent commentator on welfare and family issues. The following remarks are excerpted from his testimony before the House Ways and Means Subcommittee on Human Resources on 20 January 1995.

. . . My own view is that ending welfare is prudent and humane—prudent because the social science evidence is in: illegitimacy is the surest road to poverty and social decay. And welfare subsidizes and sustains illegitimacy. It is humane because, again, many more people would live far better lives if we scrapped an entire system that subsidizes out-of-wedlock births. Here's "tough love" on a large scale: end welfare, and young girls considering having a baby out of wedlock would face more deterrents, greater social stigma and more economic penalties arrayed against them if they have babies.

There would, therefore, be far fewer births to unwed mothers, and far greater life opportunities for those girls.

I applaud the new Republican majority for taking serious steps toward dismantling the current welfare system. That you are willing to re-examine the core assumptions of current welfare, the welfare proposal outlined in the "Contract for America," I believe is a good start. It is far better than what we have now.

There are a number of sound policy options from which to choose. I would very much like to see a radical devolution of power—that is, return power, money and responsibility back to the states, those "laboratories of democracy," where the most innovative and impressive reforms are taking place. I think that you'll agree that the governors have a far better track record than the Congress when it comes to implementing genuine welfare reform. I have outlined here some of the broad policy outlines which I would like to see states embrace. But we should give states the freedom to experiment; what works in Utah, after all, may not work nearly as well in New York.

We are now engaged in a vigorous debate about the best means to reform welfare. But it is important that we keep in mind the end-game; namely, sometime soon we want welfare to end. When it does we can judge those policies, and their broad social implications, against reality.

Mr. Chairman, our welfare system is the most pernicious government program of the past quarter century. (It is also, ironically, one of the most well-intentioned.) We have lost large parts of an entire generation because of the terrible human wreckage left in its wake. Enough is enough. It's time to pull the plug. For the sake of the children.

Let's get to it.

**Source:** House of Representatives.

# Material from Other Organizations and Individuals

## Coalition on Human Needs Welfare Reform Task Force Principles

The Coalition on Human Needs [CHN] is an alliance of over 100 national organizations working together to promote public policies which address the needs of low-income Americans. The Coalition's members include civil rights, religious, labor, and professional organizations and those concerned with the well-being of children, women, the elderly, and people with disabilities. In 1992, CHN formed a Welfare Reform Task Force composed of CHN organizations that share a strong interest in welfare policy.

CHN's Welfare Reform Task Force believes that certain fundamental principles must guide any welfare reform initiative. We believe that to properly address human needs welfare reform must: reduce the need for welfare, affirm that Americans work for wages not for welfare, and assure an adequate safety net for children and their families.

### Reduce the Need for Welfare

Reform of the Aid to Families with Dependent Children (AFDC) program cannot succeed in the absence of a broader anti-poverty strategy. Families are often forced to rely on welfare because other societal systems have failed. A meaningful anti-poverty strategy must include assured child support benefits for all children with an absent parent, improved unemployment insurance protection, a refundable children's tax credit, universal access to health care, an increased minimum wage, an expanded Earned Income Tax Credit, quality child care needed for employment and preparation for employment, as well as other reforms and initiatives outside the AFDC system.

Investing in education and training opportunities for welfare recipients is critically important. Federal funding for the Job Opportunities and Basic Skills (JOBS) program—or any successor program—should be increased to expand education and training services that give participants the necessary skills to obtain a decent paying, stable job. The state matching funding requirement should be waived or substantially reduced. Job preparation activities for AFDC recipients should include the option to pursue higher education and nontraditional training for women.

AFDC parents trying to get work and get off welfare face the realities of a labor market that is increasingly dominated by low-wage, part-time, and temporary jobs that cannot support a family. In many poor communities, jobs of any kind are scarce. Initiatives to create jobs paying a living wage must be pursued aggressively.

## Work for Wages Not for Welfare

Any public sector employment created for people leaving the AFDC system must provide pay and benefits equal to other workers doing the same work, without displacing current workers and jobs. Requiring work in exchange for welfare benefits would create a permanent class of impoverished parents who would not enjoy the basic rights to which all other American workers are entitled. Creating such a permanent working underclass would erode both wages and employment standards for all Americans.

The AFDC system should promote, not penalize, work effort. Reforms should be made to make it easier to combine some paid employment with AFDC receipt by finding ways to allow recipients to retain more of their earnings and to save for future needs.

### Assure an Adequate Safety Net for Children and Their Families

Curtailing access to welfare without reducing the need for income support will only increase poverty and hurt needy families. Time limits on the receipt of AFDC benefits are unacceptably arbitrary because they fail to take into account individual circumstances, the needs of dependent children, and the failure of the economy to generate decent jobs.

The welfare system should provide adequate support to families while they are unable to support themselves and while they are preparing to succeed in the work force. Adequate support for welfare recipients must include the income necessary to meet basic needs, as well as access to health care, housing, education or job training, child care, and other supportive services. Supportive services should be continued during periods of combining paid employment and AFDC receipt, as well as for a transitional period after receipt of AFDC ends.

While innovative strategies proposed by the states for addressing the needs of welfare recipients should be considered, state requests for waivers from federal law governing the AFDC program must be carefully reviewed by the Health and Human Services Department in a fair and public process. Some states have used the waiver process as a back-door method for cutting benefits and imposing punitive behavioral requirements on recipients. Care must be taken to prevent recipients from being worse off by waivers granted.

The welfare system must treat people with dignity. Family cap provisions, restrictions on migration and other measures that seek to punish certain behaviors hurt needy families and do nothing to help them escape poverty. A reformed welfare system should emphasize incentives over penalties.

**Source:** Coalition on Human Needs, Washington, D.C.

## An Open Letter to President Clinton

This letter was written by Children's Defense Fund founder and leader Marian Wright Edelman. It appeared in the 3 November 1995 *Washington Post*. Excerpts are reprinted below.

DO NOT ABANDON CHILDREN!
As President, you have the opportunity and personal responsibility to protect children from unjust policies. It would be a great moral and practical wrong for you to sign any welfare "reform" bill that will push millions of already poor children and families deeper into poverty as both the Senate and House welfare bills will do. It would be wrong to destroy the 60-year-old

guaranteed safety net for children, women, and poor families as both the Senate and the House welfare bills will do. It would be wrong to leave millions of voteless, voiceless children to the vagaries of 50 state bureaucracies and politics as both the Senate and House bills will do. It would be wrong to strip children of or weaken current assured help for their daily survival and during economic recessions and natural disasters as both the Senate and House bills will do. It would be wrong to exacerbate rather than alleviate the current shameful and epidemic child poverty that no decent, rich nation should tolerate for even one child.

We want to "end welfare as we know it." But we do not want to replace it with welfare as we do not want to know it. We do not want to codify a policy of national child abandonment.

# Historical Viewpoints

## The Children's Charter

President [Herbert] Hoover's White House Conference on Child Health and Protection: Recognizing the Rights of the Child as the First Rights of Citizenship, Pledges Itself to the Aims for the Children of America

For every child, spiritual and moral training to help him to stand firm under the pressure of life.

For every child, understanding and the guarding of his personality as his most precious right.

For every child, a home and that love and security which a home provides; and for that child who must receive foster care, the nearest substitute for his own home.

For every child, full preparation for his birth, his mother receiving prenatal, natal, and postnatal care; and the establishment of such protective measures as will make child-bearing safer.

For every child, health protection from birth through adolescence, including: periodical health examinations and, where needed, care of specialists and hospital treatment; regular dental examination and care of the teeth; protective and preventive measures against communicable diseases; the insuring of pure food, pure milk, and pure water.

For every child, from birth through adolescence, promotion of health, including health instruction and a health program, wholesome physical and mental recreation, with teachers and leaders adequately trained.

For every child, a dwelling place safe, sanitary, and wholesome, with reasonable provisions for privacy, free from conditions which tend to thwart his development; and a home environment harmonious and enriching.

For every child, a school which is safe from hazards, sanitary, properly equipped, lighted and ventilated. For younger children nursery schools and kindergartens to supplement home care.

For every child, a community which recognizes and plans for his needs, protects him against physical dangers, moral hazards, and disease; provides him with safe and wholesome places for play and recreation; and makes provision for his cultural and social needs.

For every child, an education which, through the discovery and development of his individual abilities, prepares him for life; and through training and vocational guidance prepares him for living which will yield him the maximum of satisfaction.

For every child, such teaching and training as will prepare him for successful parenthood, homemaking, and the rights of citizenship; and, for parents, supplementary training to fit them to deal wisely with the problems of parenthood.

For every child, education for safety and protection against accidents to which modern conditions subject him—those to which he is directly exposed and those which, through loss or maiming of his parents, affect him indirectly.

For every child, who is blind, deaf, crippled, or otherwise physically handicapped, and for the child who is mentally handicapped, such measures as will early discover and diagnose his handicap, provide care and treatment, and so train him that he may become an asset to society rather than a liability. Expenses of these services should be born publicly where they cannot be privately met.

For every child, who is in conflict with society, the right to be dealt with intelligently as society's charge, not society's outcast; with the home, the school, the church, the court and the institution when needed, shaped to return him whenever possible to the normal stream of life.

For every child, the right to group up in a family with an adequate standard of living and the security of a stable income as the surest safe guard against social handicaps.

For every child, protection against labor that stunts growth, either physical or mental, that limits education, that deprives children of the right of comradeship, of play, and of joy.

For every rural child, as satisfactory schooling and health services as for the city child, and an extension to rural families of social, recreational, and cultural facilities.

To supplement the home and the school in the training of youth, and to return to them those interests of which modern life tends to cheat children, every stimulation and encouragement should be given to the extension and development of the voluntary youth organizations.

To make everywhere available these minimum protections of the health and welfare of children, there should be a district, county, or community organization for health, education, and welfare, with full-time officials, coordinating with a state-wide program which will be responsive to a nation-wide service of general information, statistics, and scientific research. This should include:

> (a) Trained, full-time public health officials, with public health nurses, sanitary inspection, and laboratory workers.
> (b) Available hospital beds.
> (c) Full-time public welfare service for the relief, aid, and guidance of children in special need due to poverty, misfortune, or behavior difficulties, and for the protection of children from abuse, neglect, exploitation, or moral hazard.

For every child, these rights, regardless of race, or color, or situation, wherever he may live under the protection of the American flag.

**Source:** President Hoover's White House Conference on Child Health and Protection, White House.

## President Franklin Roosevelt's Programs

Roosevelt called on Congress for "some safeguards against mis-
fortunes which cannot be wholly eliminated in this man-made
world of ours . . . [so that we can] provide at once security
against several of the great disturbing factors of life. . . ."
Special Message to Congress
8 June 1934

**Source:** Library of Congress.

## President John F. Kennedy on Welfare Reform

The goals of our public welfare program must be positive and
constructive. . . . [The welfare program] must stress the integrity
and preservation of the family unit. It must contribute to the attack on dependency, juvenile delinquency, family breakdown,
illegitimacy, ill health, and disability. It must reduce the incidence of these problems, prevent their occurrence and recur-
rence, and strengthen and protect the vulnerable in a highly
competitive world.

**Source:** Text of President's Message to Congress Seeking Reform in Welfare Programs, *New York Times,* 2 February 1962.

## President Ronald Reagan on Welfare Reform

We passed our reforms in Washington but change must begin
at the grassroots, on the streets where you live. And that's why
. . . I announced that we were launching a nationwide effort to
encourage citizens to join with us in finding where need exists
and then to organize volunteer programs to meet those
needs. . . . The American people understand the logic of our
approach. A recent Roper poll found a large majority believe
that government does not spend tax money for human services
as effectively as a leading private organization like the United
Way.

**Source:** President Ronald Reagan in a speech to the New York Partnership, January 1983, Republican National Committee.

# Legislation and Litigation

# 6

President Clinton signed major welfare reform legislation into law in 1996. With this action he put into motion a detailed timetable of changes in the nation's primary cash assistance entitlement program for the poor. These changes are detailed in the material in this chapter. This action by the president followed numerous unsuccessful attempts by the Congress to reform the welfare programs. More than 20 bills on the topic had been introduced in the 104th Congress, but only one gained the president's signature.

This chapter also contains information on state actions affecting welfare programs, in particular the cash assistance programs called General Assistance, General Relief, Home Relief, or similar names. These state- or county-administered welfare programs began to undergo reform several years prior to the Aid to Families with Dependent Children (AFDC) reform effort in the U.S. Congress. Information on primary themes in litigation on welfare programs is also included.

# Federal Legislation

## The Personal Responsibility and Work Opportunity Reconciliation Act of 1996

H.R. 3734, the Personal Responsibility and Work Opportunity Reconciliation Act of 1996 was passed by the 104th Congress in August 1996. President Clinton signed the bill into law on 22 August 1996. The new welfare law ends the entitlement to assistance for the poor and cuts federal funds for programs for children and families by a total of $54 billion over six years.

Representative John Kasich (R-OH) was the chief sponsor of the welfare bill, which was first introduced 27 June 1996. The bill's short title reflects the variety of federal programs affected in the legislation: Welfare and Medicaid Reform Act of 1996; Food Stamp Reform and Commodity Distribution Act of 1996; Medicaid Restructuring Act of 1996; Personal Responsibility and Work Opportunity Act of 1996; Child Care and Development Block Grant Amendments of 1996. Provisions of the new law follow.

### Assistance for Families

H.R. 3734 ends Aid to Families with Dependent Children (AFDC), the primary cash aid program for families. It also ends JOBS (Job Opportunities and Basic Skills Training programs), the work and training program for AFDC recipients and Emergency Assistance, a program of emergency help to families with children. These programs are replaced with a block grant of federal funds given to the states.

States must operate a statewide welfare program, but the programs need not be uniform across the state. Families must receive fair and equitable treatment under the programs within a state. State programs will include assistance to families, but there is no specific requirement that families be given cash assistance. States could provide vouchers or services. Programs can be administered by private charities, religious organizations, or other private entities.

### Effective Date

Effective 1 October 1996, no individual or family is entitled to receive welfare under federal law. In general, the new law and the new block grant funding take effect 1 July 1997. States may choose to begin their programs earlier by submitting a state plan to the secretary of the U.S. Department of Health and Human Services (HHS).

A summary of this state plan must be available to the public. The plan must include assurances that local governments and private sector organizations have been consulted. Local government and private organizations must have at least 45 days to submit comments on the plan.

## Funding

The new law gives states a capped block grant set at $16.4 billion nationally; this sum does not increase. The state's block grant is the equivalent of federal payments to the state in prior years for AFDC benefits, AFDC administration, Emergency Assistance, and JOBS. No more than 15 percent of the block grant can be used for administration. Additional sums are appropriated for supplemental grants to states that have high rates of population growth and that have low amounts of federal welfare spending per poor person; bonuses to "high performing" states; bonuses to states that demonstrate a net decrease in out-of-wedlock births; and loans at market interest rates to states.

At present, if caseloads go up due to a recession, federal funding can go up to meet the need. Under the new law, basic funding is capped and cannot increase. The act establishes a $2 billion contingency fund for which states can qualify if they experience high rates of unemployment or sharp increases in food stamp participation.

## Maintenance of Effort

Under current law, in order to receive federal funds for AFDC, JOBS, Emergency Assistance, and welfare-related child care, states must provide matching funds that ranged from 50–78 percent depending on the state's poverty level and on the particular program. Under the block grant, states no longer have to provide matching funds. However, states must meet a "maintenance of effort" provision that requires them to maintain some forms of state spending. To qualify for contingency funds, states must meet a 100 percent maintenance requirement.

## Guarantee of Assistance

The new act eliminates the guarantee of help to the impoverished. There is no individual entitlement to aid established by federal law.

## Work Requirements

The new act increases work requirements. Child care funds are increased. Individuals must participate in work activities within two years of receiving aid. States must meet the following work requirements: States may count parents with children under age six and working 20 hours as engaged in work. The new definition of work is narrower than under prior law. Recipients can count twelve months of vocational education toward work requirements. Only 20 percent of the caseload can count vocational education activities toward work requirements.

For any state with a waiver in effect as of the act's date of enactment, the changes made by the bill do not apply to the state for the duration of the waiver "to the extent such amendments are inconsistent with the waiver." According to HHS, at least 33 states have waivers relating to work requirements.

Adults cannot be penalized for failure to meet work requirements if their failure is based on inability to find or afford child care for a child under 6. Otherwise, states shall reduce the family's assistance by a pro rata amount (at state option, the penalty can be higher and can include termination of help to the entire family). Adults can lose Medicaid as well as cash aid.

States that fail to meet the work requirements face fiscal penalties of up to 5 percent for the first year they violate the work requirements and greater penalties in following years.

## Family Cap

There is no explicit family cap provision in the act. A family cap is therefore a state option but is not required.

## Minor Parents

Minor parents can receive block grant funds only if they are living at home or in another adult-supervised setting. They must attend high school or an alternative educational or training program as soon as their child is at least 12 weeks old.

## Time Limit

Federal funds can be used to provide a total of five years of aid in a lifetime to a family (except that states may give hardship exemptions to up to 20 percent of their average monthly caseload). Generally, states must continue providing Medicaid to families that would be eligible for AFDC under the terms that applied on 16 July 1996, including the rules for determining income and resources. This means that families that would have qualified for AFDC under old guidelines but that lose cash aid because of new block provisions (such as the five-year time limit or lower eligibility guidelines) will at least continue to qualify for Medicaid. States may deny Medicaid to adults who lose aid because they do not meet work requirements.

### Child Care

The act eliminates the guarantee under current law that child care help will be provided to families on welfare that need child care to participate in work or training and to former welfare families that previously received one year of transitional child care help if they were able to get off welfare due to employment earnings. It also eliminates the special category of "At Risk" child care, which helped families that would be at risk of having to go on welfare if they did not get child care help. In place of these programs, the act combines new child care funding with the existing Child Care and Development Block Grant (CCDBG).

### Food Stamps

The act cuts $23 billion from the Food Stamp program over 6 years (not including cuts to legal immigrants). It reduces food stamp help for millions of poor families with children that pay more than 50 percent of their income for housing by capping the Food Stamp deduction for shelter costs. Under current law, excess shelter costs of families with children would have been taken into account in calculating the amount of Food Stamps they received. Adjustments to the Thrifty Food Plan, a low-cost food budget that is used to calculate the amount of food stamps a family receives, will reduce aid to millions more. Childless, nondisabled individuals aged 18–50 can receive only 3 months of food stamp help in a 3-year period unless they are working or participating in a workfare program at least 20 hours per week (except that they can get an additional 3 months of help, for a total of 6 months of aid, if they subsequently go to work and lose their job during that 3-year period).

### Child Nutrition Programs

The act cuts close to $3 billion over six years from child nutrition programs. These cuts include reductions in the Child and Adult Care Food Program (CACFP), including reduced nutrition aid to family day care providers who do not operate within a low-income geographic area or who are not themselves from low-income families.

## Supplemental Security Income

The act establishes a new definition of childhood disability, limiting SSI to children who meet a set of official conditions called the medical listings. The use of assessments of a child's functioning and references to maladaptive behavior are eliminated. Children who lose SSI will continue to receive Medicaid only if they are eligible on other grounds.

## Immigrant Children

The act cuts billions of dollars of help for legal aliens, including children. Effective immediately, legal aliens now in the country may not receive SSI or food stamp help (even if they currently receive these benefits). They will lose this help as soon as their cases are reviewed. At state option, as of 1 January 1997, legal aliens may also be denied welfare help, social services, and nonemergency Medicaid.

During the first five years after entry, legal aliens are barred from receiving most nonemergency means-tested federal help (including child care, Food Stamps, SSI, and welfare). After the first five years, the general rule in determining eligibility for means-tested federal programs is that the income of the legal alien's sponsor will be deemed available to the alien until the alien becomes a citizen.

## Child Support

The act makes changes to move states toward centralized and automated systems to assist in locating noncustodial parents and to begin enforcement actions automatically. The act creates registries of both national and state new hire reporting, so that child support withholding can begin when a noncustodial parent changes jobs. It requires states to report child support delinquencies to credit bureaus without waiting for a request to do so. It requires states to have the authority to withhold, suspend, or restrict the use of drivers' licenses, professional and occupational licenses, and some recreational licenses. It bolsters federal services to locate parents across state lines. It requires all states to have in place common paternity procedures in interstate cases.

The act ends the $50 child support pass-through that previously gave children on welfare at least some benefit from child support paid on their behalf. It gives children formerly on welfare priority over the state in most instances when back child support is collected and support is owed both to the child and to the state. In general, the general rule is that the new child support provisions take effect 1 October 1996.

### Title XX Social Services Block Grant

The act cuts 15 percent of funding for the Social Services Block Grant. While it allows states to transfer up to 10 percent of the welfare block grant into the Social Services Block Grant, such a transfer could be made only at the expense of reduced cash aid for children and families.

### Child Protection Programs

Federal guarantees of foster care and adoption assistance and Medicaid for foster and adopted children are generally maintained under the act. A child's eligibility for foster care and adoption assistance will be based on the eligibility of the child's family for AFDC (according to rules in effect on 1 June 1995).

# State Legislation

## General Assistance Programs

General Assistance (GA) programs are operated by some states and counties to provide aid to individuals who are not eligible for federal income assistance programs. GA programs do not receive any federal funds and are not governed by any federal standards or regulations. The state or local government that operates the program determines benefit levels, eligibility criteria, duration of assistance, and other aspects of the program.

GA programs, which are not mandatory, are funded solely by state and local government. They cover different groups of people in different states; some states offer more coverage than others. Some cover all able-bodied adults without children, while some cover two-parent families with children or people with disabilities not severe enough to qualify them for Supplemental Security Income (SSI). Some states provide benefits only to those awaiting an eligibility determination for the SSI program. Some states require GA recipients to participate in public or private employment to earn the value of their assistance.

Because GA programs are often available to single people, they are a source of income for homeless adults in many places. However, benefits are very low and are not adequate to secure housing and other necessities.

Many programs have been cut recently, and many states have sought to restrict or cut benefits for persons considered "employable." In 1991 and 1992, GA programs were reduced more than other programs for low-income people. Fourteen states cut their programs in 1991, and eight states cut programs in 1992. About 450,000 people were affected by these cuts in 1991 and 120,000 more people were affected in 1992.

## Litigation on Welfare Programs

Litigation on welfare programs has occurred at both the federal and state levels. This reflects the fact that federal welfare programs involve both federal law and regulation, and also state law and regulation. Litigation on welfare programs is often complex and technical and illustrates a variety of issues.

Some of the federal law claims involved in welfare litigation include limiting cutbacks in AFDC payment levels; federal AFDC regulations on individual advance notice; federal law governing AFDC demonstration projects; and federal constitutional claims.

State law claims involved in welfare litigation include state constitutional and statutory provisions concerning the appropriations process; state administrative procedure acts; notice and comment procedures; and state constitutional and statutory provisions concerning need standards, benefit levels, and substantive requirements.

Several helpful resources are available to assist researchers in pursuing more detailed information on both past and current litigation. These are listed in Chapter 8 (Print Resources).

# Directory of Organizations, Associations, and Government Agencies

7

The vast majority of organizations interested in issues of welfare reform are either government organizations at the federal or state level or non-profit organizations. In general, governmental organizations tend to carry out policies established by legislative bodies, while non-profit organizations tend to work towards influencing the development of or changes in those policies. This chapter lists some of the most important of these organizations.

## Non-Profit Organizations and Associations

**Judge David L. Bazelon Center
for Mental Health Law**
1100 Fifteenth Street, NW, Suite 1212
Washington, DC 20005
*Leonard Rubenstein, Executive Director*
Tel: (202) 467-5730
Fax: (202) 223-0409

The Bazelon Center is a legal advocacy organization for the rights of mentally disabled people, as well as disability programs such as SSI. The Center provides technical assistance and public education.

*Publications: Update,* published six times a year; *Community Watch.*

**Center for Community Change**
1000 Wisconsin Avenue, NW
Washington, DC 20007
*Pablo Eisenberg, President*
Tel: (202) 342-0519
Fax: (202) 342-1132

The Center provides technical assistance in the areas of Community Development Block Grants (CDBG), Community Reinvestment Act (CRA), housing trust funds, organizational development, funding, housing, and economic development for local low income community-based organizations.

*Publications: Community Change,* a quarterly newsletter.

**Center for Law and Social Policy (CLASP)**
1616 P Street NW, Suite 105
Washington, DC 20036
*Alan Houseman, Executive Director*
Tel: (202) 328-5140
Fax: (202) 328-5195
Home Page: epn.org/clasp.html

CLASP is a national public interest organization focusing on the economic condition of low-income families with children. CLASP uses education, policy research, and advocacy to advance legal and policy change at both the state and federal levels.

*Publications: Family Matters,* quarterly; *CLASP Update,* on income support issues; numerous reports; audio tapes.

**Center on Budget and Policy Priorities**
777 North Capitol Street NE, Suite 705
Washington, DC 20002
*Robert Greenstein, Director*
Tel: (202) 408-1080
Fax: (202) 408-1056
Home Page: epn.org/cbpp.html

The Center issues many reports analyzing data and policy issues affecting poor Americans; reports on poverty among women, minorities, and rural residents; and analysis of Federal budget issues and programs for the poor.

*Publications: Holes in the Safety Net: Poverty Programs and Policies in the States*, a national overview and fifty state reports, plus *A Place to Call Home*, a study of the housing crisis and the poor; regular bulletins and analyses of budget and program issues and proposals.

### Center on Social Welfare Policy and Law
275 Seventh Ave., 6th Floor
New York, NY 10001
*Henry Freedman, Executive Director*
Tel: (212) 633-6967
Fax: (212) 633-6371

The Center focuses on litigation and related issues in the income maintenance and benefits programs.

*Publications:* numerous technical regulatory and litigation oriented memos and reports; surveys of research sources; periodic reports on programs.

### Child Welfare League of America (CWLA)
440 First Street, NW  Suite 310
Washington, DC 20001
*David S. Liederman, Executive Director*
Tel: (202) 638-2952
Fax: (202) 638-4004

CWLA is a membership organization of children's advocacy agencies, as well as public and voluntary organizations. It is active in the areas of research, training, and legislative advocacy on children's issues, including the needs of homeless children.

*Publications: Child Welfare*, a bi-monthly journal; *Washington Social Legislation Bulletin*, a bi-weekly report, "Homeless Children and Families;" *The Youngest of the Homeless II*, a report on boarder babies.

### Children's Defense Fund (CDF)
25 E Street, NW
Washington, DC 20001
*Marian Wright Edelman, President*
Tel: (202) 628-8787

CDF's goal is to educate policymakers about the needs of poor and minority children. It monitors Federal and state policy and legislation on health, education, child welfare, mental health, teen pregnancy, and youth employment.

*Publications: CDF Reports,* published monthly as an update on relevant issues; *A Children's Defense Budget,* an annual, exhaustive analysis of Federal budget proposals and their effects on children; other specialized reports and fact books on the needs of poor and minority children.

### Christian Coalition
227 Massachusetts Ave., NE
Washington, DC 20001
*Ralph Reed, Executive Director*
Tel: (202) 547-3600

A conservative Christian organization active in social policy debate.

*Publications:* numerous analyses and bulletins on welfare and related issues.

### Coalition on Human Needs
1000 Wisconsin Avenue, NW
Washington, DC 20007
*Jennifer Vasiloff, Executive Director*
Tel: (202) 342-0726

A wide range of groups concerned with issues affecting low-income people participate in this coalition, which seeks to reduce poverty and improve the education and welfare systems. Research assistance and legislative information are provided to affiliates.

*Publications: The National Technical Assistance Directory: A Guide for State Advocates and Service Providers,* a directory of national organizations providing technical assistance and analytical publications.

### Council of State Community Development Agencies (COSCDA)
444 North Capitol Street, NE, Suite 224
Washington, DC 20001
*John M. Sidor, Executive Director*
Tel: (202) 393-6435

This national network of state-level community development officials monitors federal legislation and state initiatives on affordable housing and economic development and employment issues.

*Publications:* "States and Housing," a newsletter; *Put Up or Give Way*, a book about state jobs and employment strategies.

**Families USA**
1334 G Street NW, 3rd floor
Washington, DC 20005
*Ron Pollack, Executive Director*
Tel: (202) 628-3030

Families USA is a national public policy organization active on health care, welfare reform, and related issues.

*Publications:* numerous analyses, bulletins, and reports on legislative proposals and programs.

**Food Research and Action Center (FRAC)**
1875 Connecticut Avenue, NW, Suite 540
Washington, DC 20009
*Robert Fersh, Executive Director*
Tel: (202) 986-2200
Fax: (202) 986-2525

FRAC is a national legal services support center on food, nutrition, and hunger issues. Its primary goal is to reduce hunger in America through the improvement of federal food programs, and it acts as a clearinghouse on public policy, legislation, technical assistance, education, and the formation of statewide coalitions.

*Publications: Foodlines*, a monthly newsletter; *FRAC's Guide to the Food Stamp Program;* and *WIC Facts*.

**Heritage Foundation**
214 Massachusetts Ave., NE
Washington, DC 20001
Tel: (202) 546-4400

The Heritage Foundation is a conservative public policy organization active in the welfare reform debate and related issues.

*Publications:* numerous analyses, briefs, and proposals.

**Institute for Research on Poverty**
1180 Observatory Drive
3412 Social Science Building
University of Wisconsin
Madison, WI 53706
*Barbara L. Wolfe, Director*
Tel: (608) 262-6358
Fax: (608) 265-3119
e-mail: eunice.ssc.wisc.edu

The Institute is a university-based research center focusing on poverty. It conducts events and research and disseminates a large number of papers and publications, including a discussion paper series and a reprint series.

*Publications: FOCUS*, a newsletter published three times a year, and *INSIGHTS*, published monthly.

**National Clearinghouse for Legal Services**
205 W. Monroe, 2nd floor
Chicago, IL 60606
*Rita McLennon, Executive Director*
Tel: (312) 263-3830
Fax: (312) 263-3846

The Clearinghouse is a national center on poverty law.

*Publications: Clearinghouse Review*, a journal on poverty law.

**National Conference of State Legislatures (NCSL)**
1050 Seventeenth Street  Suite 2100
Denver, CO 80265
*William T. Pound, Executive Director*
Tel: (303) 623-7800

NCSL serves the members of the nation's fifty state legislatures through publications and other tools with current information on state and federal public policy issues.

*Publications: State Legislatures*, published ten times annually; *Federal Update*, a newsletter; *State Legislative Report*, a policy update; and *Directory of Legislative Leaders*, a national guide.

**National Governors' Association (NGA)**
444 North Capitol Street, NW
Washington, DC 20001

*Raymond C. Scheppach, Executive Director*
Tel: (202) 624-5300

NGA is a national organization of governors of the states that has been a key participant in the welfare reform debate.

*Publications:* several summaries of state actions, proposals, and legislation on AFDC and General Assistance programs.

**United States Conference of Mayors**
1620 Eye Street, NW
Washington, DC 20005
*Laura DeKoven Waxman, Assistant Executive Director*
Tel: (202) 293-7330
Fax: (202) 293-2352

The Conference of Mayors is an educational and lobbying organization for mayors of cities over 30,000 population. It provides background information and position statements on vital issues. Its Task Force on Hunger and Homelessness conducts an annual survey of member cities and their services and conditions.

*Publications: The Continued Growth of Hunger, Homelessness, and Poverty in America's Cities,* an annual report.

# Federal Agencies

**Bureau of the Census**
Department of Commerce
Washington, DC 20233
Tel: (301) 763-4040

The Bureau produces numerous statistical resources on income and poverty in the nation.

**Department of Agriculture (USDA)**
Fourteenth Street and Independence Avenue, SW
Washington, DC 20250
Tel: (202) 447-2791

Through the Food and Nutrition Service, the USDA administers the Food Stamp and McKinney Act regulations.

**Department of Health and Human Services (HHS)**
200 Independence Avenue, SW

Washington, DC 20201
Tel: (202) 619-0257

HHS administers the AFDC programs and many other benefits programs for poor people.

**Department of Housing and Urban Development (HUD)**
451 Seventh Street, SW
Washington, DC 20410
Tel: (202) 708-1422

HUD administers a variety of low-income housing programs and self-sufficiency programs for poor people in public and assisted housing.

**Department of Labor**
200 Constitution Avenue, NW
Washington, DC 20210
Tel: (202) 523-8165

The Department of Labor administers many job training and related programs for poor and disadvantaged persons.

**Social Security Administration**
6401 Security Boulevard
Baltimore, MD 21235
Tel: (410) 965-7700
Fax: (410) 966-1337

The SSA administers the SSI and other income programs for needy persons.

# Print Resources 8

What is the function of governments in addressing poverty? That question has been discussed and debated in the United States for more than two centuries. Throughout that period, some individuals and some organizations have felt that policies and practices then in existence were inappropriate and needed reform. The issue of welfare reform in the 1990s is hardly a new question.

This chapter lists some important print resources to which the interested reader can go for further information about this long-standing debate. Books and reports dealing with the history of public welfare and welfare reform, with poverty-related issues, and with suggestions for reform are listed.

## Bibliographies

Trattner, Walter I., and W. Andrew Achenbaum. *Social Welfare in America: An Annotated Bibliography.* Westport, CT: Greenwood Press, 1983. 324 pp. ISBN 0-313-23002-1.

This bibliography is divided into six subtopics ranging from "Caring for the Infant and Child" to "Coping with the Difficulties of

Old Age." It closes with an epilogue on "An Agenda for Future Research in American Social Welfare History."

Urban Affairs Library. *NewsBank Index.* Chesterton, IN: Arcata Microfilm Corp. ISSN 0737-3813.

A monthly publication of the Urban Affairs Library listing relevant publications in the field of welfare and poverty. The publication began in 1970 as *NewsBank: Welfare and Poverty* and was merged with the general index in 1981.

## Directories

American Public Welfare Association. *The Public Welfare Directory.* Chicago: American Public Welfare Association. Published annually. ISSN 0163-8297.

Lists names, addresses, and telephone numbers of individuals and agencies in federal and state government involved in public welfare programs in the United States, Canada, and selected other nations. An appendix lists all major public welfare legislation.

## General Books

Aaron, Henry J. *Why Is Welfare So Hard To Reform?* Washington, DC: Brookings Institution, 1973. 71 pp. ISBN 0-8157-0019-9 (pbk.).

This relatively technical paper discusses the problem of the cumulative marginal tax rate, the amount by which an increase in earnings from being employed is offset by reductions in cash assistance, housing subsidies, food stamps, and other forms of public welfare.

American Enterprise Institute. *The Administration's 1979 Welfare Reform Proposal, 1979, 96th Congress, 1st Session.* Washington, DC: American Enterprise Institute, 1979. 61 pp. ISBN 0-8447-0222-6.

A good overview of major issues of the welfare system that need to be resolved (many of which are still being discussed today) along with a critique of specific features of President Carter's 1979 proposals for reform.

American Enterprise Institute. *Welfare Reform: Why?* Washington, DC: American Enterprise Institute. 41 pp. ISBN 0-8447-2087-9.

This short book is a verbatim transcript of a round-table discussion sponsored by the American Enterprise Institute, a conservative think-tank, in 1976. The participants were Abraham Ribicoff, Democratic senator from Connecticut; Barber Conable, Republican member of the House from New York State; Wilbur Cohen, dean of the School of Education at the University of Michigan; and Paul McAvoy, member of the President's Council of Economic Advisers.

Anderson, Martin. *Welfare: The Political Economy of Welfare Reform in the United States.* Stanford, CA: Hoover Institution Press, 1978. 251 pp. ISBN 0-8179-6811-3.

The author's purpose is "to examine essentials of [the] debate" over welfare reform. He provides an excellent overview of the then-current welfare system, reasons for the demands for welfare reform, and suggestions for a "workable" welfare reform effort. Appendix A of the book lists all existing public welfare programs.

Auletta, Ken. *The Underclass.* New York: Vintage Books, 1982. 336 pp. ISBN 0-3947-1388-5 (pbk.).

An early and controversial depiction of intergenerational poverty and urban problems.

Baldwin, John. *Education and Welfare Reform: The Story of a Second-Chance School.* Bloomington, IN: Phi Delta Kappa Educational Foundation, 1993. 41 pp. ISBN 0-87367-355-7 (pbk.).

The story of the creation in 1990 of the Hamilton Terrace Learning Center in Shreveport, Louisiana, as a way of helping adults on welfare from getting out of the "welfare cycle of dependency."

Bane, Mary Jo, and David T. Ellwood. *Welfare Realities: From Rhetoric to Reform.* Cambridge, MA: Harvard University Press, 1994. 220 pp. ISBN 0-674-94912-9.

A collection of papers and reports written, but not published, over the preceding decade by the authors. Each chapter attempts to "examine welfare, its recipients, its providers, and the swirl of policy ideas with calm and clarity."

Berkowitz, Edward, and Kim McQuaid. *Creating the Welfare State: The Political Economy of Twentieth-Century Reform*, revised edition. Lawrence, KS: University Press of Kansas, 1992. 247 pp. ISBN 0-7006-0528-2.

An unusually fine history of the development of the public welfare system in the United States from about 1880 to the present.

Bremner, Robert H. *The Discovery of Poverty in the United States.* New Brunswick, NJ: Transaction Publishers, 1992. 364 pp. ISBN 1-56000-582-3.

Considered a landmark book upon its release, this is an examination of the origins of American attitudes about poverty.

Brodkin, Evelyn Z. *The False Promise of Administrative Reform: Implementing Quality Control in Welfare.* Philadelphia: Temple University Press, 1986. 156 pp. ISBN 0-87722-431-5.

An analysis of President Richard Nixon's efforts to reform public welfare programs and their ultimate consequences on the poor, along with a discussion of the political conflict that developed as a result of the President's proposed reforms.

Burke, Vincent J., and Vee Burke. *Nixon's Good Deed: Welfare Reform.* New York: Columbia University Press, 1974. 243 pp. ISBN 0-231-03850-X.

An intriguing review of the political process by which Nixon's "good deed," his Family Assistance Program, was overwhelmed by bureaucratic, legislative, and practical realities that prevented the program from ever being implemented in the form that Nixon had imagined it.

Butler, Stuart, and Anna Kondratas. *Out of the Poverty Trap: A Conservative Strategy for Welfare Reform.* New York: Free Press, 1987. 264 pp. ISBN 0-02-90506-8.

After an opening chapter on "Why the War on Poverty Is Being Lost," the authors suggest the way in which a public welfare system based on conservative principles can be constructed in the United States and then go on to outline details of the way in which such a system would operate.

Citro, Constance F., and Robert T. Michael, eds. *Measuring Poverty: A New Approach.* Washington, DC: National Academy Press, 1995. 501 pp. ISBN 0-309-05128-2.

The final report of the Panel on Poverty and Family Assistance: Concepts, Information Needs, and Measurement Methods based on its 2 1/2 year investigation into questions involving the measurement of poverty and the appropriate relationship between poverty standards and AFDC need standards. Produced in response to both a provision in the Family Support Act of 1988 and a directive from the Joint Economic Committee of Congress.

*Confronting Poverty: Prescriptions for Change.* Cambridge: Harvard University Press, 1994. 530 pp. ISBN 0-674-16082-7.

Essays by some of the primary thinkers on issues of poverty, welfare, and policy.

Cottingham, Phoebe H., and David T. Ellwood, eds. *Welfare Policy for the 1990s.* Cambridge, MA: Harvard University Press, 1989. 349 pp. ISBN 0-674-94905-6.

This collection of essays discusses changes in the welfare system as proposed by President Ronald Reagan in February 1986.

Critchlow, Donald T., and Ellis W. Hawley. *Poverty and Public Policy in Modern America.* Chicago: Dorsey Press, 1989. 332 pp. ISBN 0-256-06024-X.

Arguably the most complete review of American public welfare policies and practices from the American Revolution to the late 1980s.

Cunningham, Patrick M. *Welfare Reform: A Response to Unemployed Two-Parent Families.* New York: Garland Publishing Company, 1993. 160 pp. ISBN 0-8153-1114-1.

The author reports on his study of the Utah Emergency Work Program, designed to provide assistance for low-income families in which both parents are present. The book contains a superb and concise overview of the history of public welfare programs in the United States.

Danziger, Sheldon H., Gary D. Sandefur, and Daniel H. Weinberg, eds. *Confronting Poverty: Prescriptions for Change.* Cambridge, MA: Harvard University Press, 1994. 529 pp. ISBN 0-674-16081-9.

The chapters in this book were originally presented at a conference held in May 1992 and sponsored jointly by the Institute for

Research on Poverty of the University of Wisconsin-Madison and the Office of the Assistant Secretary for Planning and Evaluation of the U.S. Department of Health and Human Services.

Danziger, Sheldon H. and Daniel H. Weinberg, eds. *Fighting Poverty: What Works and What Doesn't.* Cambridge, MA: Harvard University Press, 1986. 418 pp. ISBN 0-674-30086-6.

Revised versions of papers presented at a conference held in December 1984 and sponsored by the Institute for Research on Poverty of the University of Wisconsin-Madison and the U.S. Department of Health and Human Services.

Demone, Harold W., Jr., and Margaret Gibelman. *Services for Sale: Purchasing Health and Human Services.* Rutgers, NJ: Rutgers University Press, 1989. 450 pp. ISBN 0-8135-1362-6.

An examination of the history of private voluntary public welfare services and ways in which they can be utilized in current public welfare reform programs.

Ellwood, David T. *Poor Support: Poverty in the American Family.* New York: Basic Books, 1988. 270 pp. ISBN 0-465-05995-3.

In an early work that achieved influence on contemporary policy, this former Clinton administration official examines poverty and asserts many of the themes that have marked current proposals.

Esterly, Stanley, and Glenn Esterly. *Freedom from Dependence: Welfare Reform as a Solution to Poverty.* Washington, DC: Public Affairs Press, 1971. 178 pp. no ISBN.

An analysis of the "steadily deteriorating" public welfare system in the United States, along with proposals to reverse the trend and a critique of President Nixon's 1969 Family Assistance Plan.

Freedman, Jonathan. *From Cradle to Grave: The Human Face of Poverty in America.* New York: Atheneum, 1993. 245 pp. ISBN 0-689-12126-1.

A picture of some of the individuals behind the statistics and rhetoric of the antipoverty debate.

Friedlander, Daniel and Gary Burtless. *Five Years After: The Long Term Effects of Welfare-to-Work Programs.* A Manpower

Demonstration Research Corporation Study. New York: Russell Sage Foundation Books, 1994. 230 pp. ISBN 0-8715-4266-8.

This study examines four WIN demonstration projects from the 1980s (Arkansas, Virginia, San Diego, California, and Baltimore, Maryland) to determine what long term impact programs had.

Galbraith, John K. *The Affluent Society.* Boston: Houghton Mifflin, 1958. 368 pp. no ISBN.

An early work asserting the achievement of affluence in the U.S. and the relative lack of poverty.

Gaylin, Willard, ed. *Doing Good: The Limits of Benevolence.* New York: Pantheon Books, 1978. 171 pp. ISBN 0-394-41133-1.

A professor of history, a professor of comparative literature, a psychoanalyst, and the director of the New York State chapter of the American Civil Liberties Union explore the issue of public welfare as a mechanism for dealing with human dependency.

Gilder, George. *Wealth and Poverty.* New York: Basic Books, 1980. 295 pp. ISBN 0-465-09105-9.

Golden, Olivia. *Poor Children and Welfare Reform.* Westport, CT: Auburn House, 1992. 193 pp. ISBN 0-86569-045-6.

The author reports on seven welfare agencies in the United States that are regarded as being "successful" in meeting the needs of children and the job-related needs of mothers. She then makes recommendations for the broader development of such programs based on her study.

Goodman, Roy M. *The Administration's Welfare Reform Proposal: A Costly Mistake: A Report.* Albany, NY: Legislative Commission on Public-Private Cooperation, May 1986. 74 pp. no ISBN.

The chair of the New York State Legislative Commission on Public-Private Cooperation provides an interesting critique of Governor Mario Cuomo's proposals to reform the State's public welfare program.

Gordon, Linda, ed. *Women, the State, and Welfare.* Madison, WI: University of Wisconsin Press, 1990. 311 pp. ISBN 0-299-12644-1.

A collection of articles examining the role of gender in the development, operation, and goals of welfare programs.

Gueron, Judith, and Edward Pauly. *From Welfare to Work.* New York: Manpower Demonstration Research Corporation, 1991. 316 pp. ISBN 0-87154-346-X.

An examination by the leading authority on employment programs for welfare recipients of the outcomes in programs designed to move AFDC beneficiaries through work programs.

Handler, Joel F. *The Moral Construction of Poverty: Welfare Reform in America.* Newbury Park, NY: Sage Publications, 1991. 269 pp. ISBN 0-8039-4198-6 (pbk.).

An analysis of moral and ethical issues involved in the reform of public welfare programs in the United States.

Handler, Joel F. *The Poverty of Welfare Reform.* New Haven, CT: Yale University Press, 1995. 177 pp. ISBN 0-300-06480-2.

The author discusses current calls for reform of the public welfare system by both President Clinton and the Republican Congress and shows how these demands fit into a long historical pattern in which welfare policy is not addressed as a way of aiding poor people, but "an affirmation of majoritarian values through the creation of deviants [the poor]."

Harrington, Michael. *The Other America: Poverty in the United States.* New York: Macmillan Company, 1962. 221 pp. ISBN 0-14-02-1308-2.

The classic study of poverty in the U.S. that set in the motion the Kennedy-Johnson era policies of the War on Poverty.

Hoffman, Wayne Lee. *Work Incentives and Implicit Tax Rates in the Carter Welfare Reform Plan, with a Comparison to Current Policy.* Washington, DC: Urban Institute, 1977. 46 pp. ISBN 0-87766-212-6.

One of a series of reports analyzing President Carter's welfare reform program.

*In the Shadow of the Poorhouse: A Social History of Welfare in America.* New York: Basic Books, 1986. 338 pp. ISBN 0-465-03226-5.

Traces the evolution of American approaches to studying and remedying poverty and changing the behavior of the poor.

Jencks, Christopher and Kathryn Edin. *The Urban Underclass.* Washington, DC: The Brookings Institution, 1991. 490 pp. ISBN 0-8157-4606-7.

Pays particular attention to issues involving race and urban problems.

Jencks, Christopher. *Rethinking Social Policy: Race, Poverty, and the Underclass.* New York: Harper, 1992. 280 pp. ISBN 0-06-097534-2.

Examines American thinking about race and poverty issues as well as other major books on these topics.

Jennings, Edward T., Jr., and Neal S. Zank. *Welfare System Reform: Coordinating Federal, State, and Local Public Assistance Programs.* Westport, CT: Greenwood Press, 1993. 249 pp. ISBN 0-313-28485-7.

A report on a two-year study by the National Commission for Employment Policy, whose charge it was to recommend approaches for coordinating the many disparate elements of welfare reform at various governmental levels.

Johnson, Bruce S. *The Reluctant Welfare State: A History of American Social Welfare Policies.* Belmont, CA: Wadsworth Press, 1988. 278 pp. ISBN 0-53408-490-7.

A complete and extensive history of public welfare policies and practices in the United States.

Katz, Michael B. *The Undeserving Poor: From the War on Poverty to the War on Welfare.* New York: Pantheon Books, 1989. 293 pp. ISBN 0-679-72561-x.

The author is considered a prime historian of social welfare in the U.S. Here he examines the theme of the "deserving" and the "undeserving" poor.

Leman, Christopher. *The Collapse of Welfare Reform: Political Institutions, Policy, and the Poor in Canada and the United States.* Cambridge, MA: MIT Press, 1980. 292 pp. ISBN 0-262-12081-X.

This book takes the somewhat unusual approach of comparing welfare reform efforts in the United States and Canada during the 1970s, finding quite surprising differences in the directions taken in the two countries.

Levitan, Sar A. *Programs in Aid of the Poor.* Baltimore: Johns Hopkins University Press, 1990. 189 pp. ISBN 0-8018-4040-6.

Levitan, Sar A., Frank Gallo, and Isaac Shapiro. *Working but Poor.* Baltimore: The Johns Hopkins University Press, 1993. 152 pp. ISBN 0-8018-4575-0.

Examines the working poor in America, and the income and tax policies, as well as minimum wages provisions, that have combined with inadequate employment and training programs to address changes in job markets, globalization, growth of technology, and income supports.

Levy, Frank. *The Logic of Welfare Reform.* Washington, DC: Urban Institute Press, 1980. 81 pp. ISBN 0-87766-282-7.

A concise and readable discussion of the public welfare system as it existed in 1980, with a review of reasons that reforms were then necessary, problems to be faced in achieving those reforms, and strategies to explore for reform in the future.

Liebow, Elliot. *Tell Them Who I Am: The Lives of Homeless Women.* New York: Free Press, 1993. 339 pp. ISBN 0-02-919095-9.

Long, Robert Emmet, ed. *The Welfare Debate.* New York: Wilson Company, 1989. 205 pp. ISBN 0-8242-0782-3.

A superb collection of essays that present the pros and cons of the welfare reform debate, largely instigated by President Ronald Reagan's welfare reform proposals of the 1980s.

Lynn, Laurence E. *The President as Policymaker: Jimmy Carter and Welfare Reform.* Philadelphia: Temple University Press, 1981. 351 pp. ISBN 0-87722-223-1.

This very detailed examination of efforts by President Carter to reform the public welfare system was used as a case study in the author's classes at the John F. Kennedy School of Government at Harvard.

Mandell, Betty Reid, ed. *Welfare in America: Controlling the "Dangerous Classes."* Englewood Cliffs, NJ: Prentice-Hall, 1975. 186 pp. ISBN 0-1394-9313-1.

The text argues that the welfare system is not so much a mechanism for helping the poor as it is for keeping them in their place and for maintaining the vested interests of those who run welfare programs.

Mead, Lawrence M. *Beyond Entitlement: The Social Obligations of Citizenship.* New York: Free Press, 1986. 307 pp. ISBN 0-029-20890-4.

Mead, Lawrence M. *The New Politics of Poverty: The Nonworking Poor in America.* New York: Basic Books, 1992. 356 pp. ISBN 0-465-05962-7.

Miller, Dorothy C. *Women and Social Welfare: A Feminist Analysis.* New York: Praeger Books, 1992. 181 pp. ISBN 0-275-94384-4.

Morris, Robert. *Rethinking Social Welfare: Why Care for the Stranger?* New York: Longman, 1986. 275 pp. ISBN 0-582-28589-5 (pbk.).

The three parts of this book deal with the status of public welfare programs in the United States in the 1980s, the history of public welfare extending as far back as Biblical times, and alternatives for the future.

Moynihan, Daniel P. *Family and Nation.* San Diego: Harcourt Brace Jovanovich, 1986. 197 pp. ISBN 0-1513-0143-3.

A reprint of Moynihan's Godkin Lectures, delivered at Harvard University in 1985.

Moynihan, Daniel P. *The Politics of a Guaranteed Income: The Nixon Administration and the Family Assistance Plan.* New York: Vintage Books, 1973. 579 pp. ISBN 0-3947-1931-X.

The guaranteed minimum income proposal of the Nixon administration and its encouragement of work are examined here by one of the foremost proponents of the plan and a recognized expert in welfare in the U.S. Senate.

Murray, Charles. *Losing Ground: American Social Policy, 1950-1980.* New York: Basic Books, 1984. 322 pp. ISBN 0-465-04232-5.

Argues the conservative view that the War on Poverty programs of the 1960s not only failed to help poor people but actually caused harm by creating dependency and a culture of welfare.

*The New American Poverty.* New York: Penguin Books, 1984. 271 pp. ISBN 0-14-008112-7.

An examination of poverty in the 1980s, including the extent of homelessness in the U.S.

Newman, Sandra J., and Ann B. Schnare. *Subsidizing Shelter: The Relationship between Welfare and Housing Assistance.* Washington, DC: Urban Institute Press, 1988. 193 pp. ISBN 0-87766-414-5. Part 1: Analysis and Findings. Part 2: Data Book.

Welfare recipients receive at least $10 billion annually for housing assistance, funds that are part of their public assistance benefits. The HUD stream of funding for low-income housing is about the same, yet the relationship between the two programs is largely unexamined and their effects uncoordinated.

Nightingale, Demetra Smith, and Robert H. Haveman, eds. *The Work Alternative: Welfare Reform and the Realities of the Job Market.* Washington, DC: Urban Institute Press, 1995. 218 pp. ISBN 0-87766-623-7.

A collection of papers presented at a conference on proposals for finding employment for people on welfare. Major issues addressed were whether the jobs needed for such an approach are actually available and whether such jobs pay enough to get people off welfare.

Novak, Michael, et al. *The New Consensus on Family and Welfare.* Washington, DC: American Enterprise Institute, 1987.

Examines the conservative view of the value of work and family in light of the welfare system.

Patterson, James T. *America's Struggle against Poverty, 1900-1994.* Cambridge, MA: Harvard University Press, 1994. 309 pp. ISBN 0-674-03123-7.

The second revision of a book originally published in 1981 providing a superb historical and analytical review of social welfare programs in the United States. The book is especially interesting and valuable because of its attention to recurring themes such as beliefs that the destitute are undeserving, the intergenerational culture of poverty, the assumption that welfare is wasteful and demoralizing, and the belief that work and not welfare is the "essence of a meaningful life."

Pechman, Joseph A., ed. *Fulfilling America's Promise: Social Policies for the 1990s.* Ithaca, NY: Cornell University Press, 1992. 260 pp. ISBN 0-8014-8059-0.

Presents ideas on how to craft policies that assist the poor and other groups in the decade of the 1990s.

Phillips. Kevin. *The Politics of Rich and Poor: Wealth and the Aftermath of the Reagan Election.* New York: Random House, 1990. 263 pp. ISBN 0-394-55954-1.

An expert political analyst examines the increasing gulf in income in the U.S. and its effect on electoral politics.

Piven, Frances Fox, and Richard A. Cloward. *Regulating the Poor: The Functions of Public Welfare.* New York: Vintage Books, 1993. 524 pp. ISBN 0-679-74516-5.

The authors are known as analysts of the welfare system from their work with client organizations. Here they examine the ways in which the welfare system has other effects in the lives of those who come into contact with it.

Reischauer, Robert D. *The Impact of Social Welfare Policies in the United States.* New York: The Conference Board, 1982. 26 pp. ISBN 0-8237-0260-X.

An excellent review of then-current public welfare policies and programs, with a discussion of policy issues and the potential impact of President Ronald Reagan's recommended changes in welfare policy. The author was later to become President Bill Clinton's Secretary of Labor.

Schwartz, John E., and Thomas J. Volgy. *The Forgotten Americans: Thirty Million Working Poor in the Land of Opportunity.* New York: W.W. Norton, 1992. 219 pp. ISBN 0-393-03388-0.

Studies the segment of the American work force that has full-time year-round work, but does not rise out of poverty.

Sheehan, Susan. *Life for Me Ain't Been No Crystal Stair.* New York: Pantheon, 1993. 175 pp. ISBN 0-679-41472-x.

An author noted for careful portrayals of her subjects looks at a multi-generational family experiencing poverty and public efforts to remedy it.

Sommers, Paul M., ed. *Welfare Reform in America: Perspectives and Prospects.* Boston: Kluwer-Nijhoff, 1982.

Report of the 1980 Middlebury College Conference on Economic Issues that analyzed President Nixon's Family Assistance Plan and President Carter's Program for Better Jobs and Income. The participants also proposed a number of ideas regarding future reform of the public welfare system.

*The States, the People and the Reagan Years: An Analysis of Social Spending Cuts.* Washington, DC: American Federation of State, County and Municipal Employees, 1984. ca. 200 pp. No ISBN.

This volume reports on "a four-year, program-by-program and state-by-state analysis of the social spending cuts enacted since FY 1981, including President Reagan's proposed cuts for FY 1985." It consists chiefly of tables showing the loss of federal aid in various categories and geographical areas. The report also includes a listing of existing public welfare programs.

Storey, James R. *The Better Jobs and Income Plan: A Guide to President Carter's Welfare Reform Proposal and Major Issues.* Washington, DC: Urban Institute, 1978. 97 pp. ISBN 087766-213-4.

One of a series of reports published by the Urban Institute critiquing President Carter's 1978 welfare proposals, including a description of the proposals, possible alternatives, and "larger issues" of welfare reform.

Sulvetta, Margaret B. *The Impact of Welfare Reform on Benefits for the Poor: A Comparison of Eligibility Requirements and Benefit Levels under the Proposed Program for Better Jobs and Income and the Current System.* Washington, DC: Urban Institute, 1978. 52 pp. ISBN 0-87766-218-5 (pbk.).

One of a series of reports by the Urban Institute analyzing President's Carter's proposed welfare reform proposals.

*The "Underclass" Debate: Views from History.* Princeton, NJ: Princeton University Press, 1993. 506 pp. ISBN 0-691-00628-8.

Essays reflecting the longstanding controversy about the poor and how best to aid them.

Weir, Margaret, Ann Shola Orloff, and Theda Skokpol. *The Politics of Social Policy in the United States.* Princeton, NJ: Princeton University Press, 1988. 465 pp. ISBN 0-69109-436-5.

Revisions of papers originally presented at an on-going conference held in Chicago and sponsored by the Project on the Federal Social Role.

*Welfare Reform: Why?* Washington, DC: American Enterprise Institute. 41 pp. ISBN 0-8447-2087-9.

This short book is a verbatim transcript of a round-table discussion sponsored by the American Enterprise Institute, a conservative think-tank, in 1976. The participants were Abraham Ribicoff, Democratic senator from Connecticut; Barber Conable, Republican member of the House from New York State; Wilbur Cohen, dean of the School of Education at the University of Michigan; and Paul McAvoy, member of the President's Council of Economic Advisors.

Wilson, William Julius. *The Truly Disadvantaged: The Inner City, the Underclass, and Public Policy.* Chicago: University of Chicago Press, 1987. 254 pp. ISBN 0-226-90130-0.

Considered an important examination of urban and long-term poverty and possible policy directions for remedying these problems.

Wong, Pat. *Child Support and Welfare Reform.* New York: Garland Publishing Company, 1993. 184 pp. ISBN 0-8153-1123-0.

A re-working of the author's Ph.D. thesis analyzing then-current child welfare policies and outlining changes in that policy that would "enforce the social values that it is supposed to embody."

# Reports (Governmental Agencies)

*Block Grants: Characteristics, Experience, and Lessons Learned.* Washington, DC: U.S. General Accounting Office, 1995. GAO/HEHS-95-74.

This report examines previous GAO reports on the consolidation of 50 categorical programs into block grants in 1981.

*Characteristics of State Plans for the Job Opportunities and Basic Skills Training (JOBS) Program.* Washington, DC: Department of Health and Human Services.

This document is published biannually and based on information in the state JOBS plan which each state must submit to HHS every two years. Part I is organized state-by-state, and Part II contains information organized characteristic-by-characteristic.

*Child Care: Child Care Subsidies Increase Likelihood that Low-Income Mothers Will Work.* Washington, DC: General Accounting Office, December 1994. 35 pp. GAO/HEHS-95-20.

Demonstrates that the role of reliable child care is crucial in the work-to-welfare plans of single mothers in poverty.

*Child Care: Current Systems Could Undermine Goals of Welfare Reform.* Washington, DC: General Accounting Office, 1994. 43 pp. GAO/T-HEHS-94-238.

An examination of the flaws in present child care programs and their potential for thwarting welfare-to-work efforts.

*Child Care: Narrow Subsidy Programs Create Problems for Mothers Trying to Work.* Washington, DC: General Accounting Office, 1995. 17 pp. GAO/T-HEHS-95-69.

Existing subsidy programs for poor mothers are too tightly constructed to provide real opportunity for those making the welfare-to-work transition.

*Child Care: Working Poor and Welfare Recipients Face Service Gaps.* Washington, DC: General Accounting Office, May 1994. 19 pp. GAO/HEHS-94-87.

Reviews state implementation of the child care block grants to determine what problems states encounter with the programs, as well as gaps in child care delivery for low income people.

*Child Support Enforcement: Families Could Benefit from Stronger Enforcement Program.* Washington, DC: General Accounting Office, December 1994. 116 pp. GAO/HEHS-95-24.

Examines how the federal government can improve child support enforcement services to the states and needy families.

*Child Support Enforcement: States Proceed with Immediate Wage Withholding; More HHS Action Needed.* Washington, DC: General Accounting Office, June 1993. 25 pp. GAO/HRD-93-99.

Wage related actions are one of the ways in which unpaid child support is collected. This report looks at additional ways such efforts could be made.

*Child Welfare: HHS Begins to Assume Leadership to Implement National and State Systems.* Washington, DC: General Accounting Office, June 1994. 45 pp. GAO/AIMD-94-37.

Surveys HHS actions in meeting goals for child welfare systems.

*Child Welfare: Opportunities to Further Enhance Family Preservation and Support Activities.* Washington, DC: General Accounting Office, June 1995. 87 pp. GAO/HEHS-95-112.

Describes the child welfare issues that produced new initiatives in preservation and support, assesses federal efforts to implement these provisions, and examines ways to enhance these efforts.

*Dynamics of Economic Well-Being: Poverty, 1990 to 1992.* Current Population Reports, Household Economic Studies, Bureau of the Census, 1995.

This report uses data from the Survey of Income and Program Participation (SIPP) to examine the incidence of poverty. The report finds that, in an average month of 1990, 31.8 million persons were poor, representing 12.9 percent of the population.

*Dynamics of Economic Well-Being: Program Participation, 1990 to 1992.* Current Population Reports, Household Economic Studies, P70-41, January 1995. Washington, DC: Bureau of the Census, 1995. 50 pp.

Data from the Survey of Income and Program Participation (SIPP) is used to examine participation in various government assistance programs.

Ellwood, D. *Understanding Dependency: Choices, Confidence or Culture?* Prepared for U.S. Department of Health and Human Services, contract no. HHS-OS-100-86-0021.

Examines the possible causes of long-term welfare receipt.

Ellwood, D. *Working Off of Welfare: Prospects and Policies for Self-Sufficiency of Women Heading Families.* Discussion Paper 803-86, Institute for Research on Poverty, University of Wisconsin-Madison.

Discusses the transition to work and some of the problems faced by AFDC recipients.

*Families on Welfare: Focus on Teenage Mothers Could Enhance Welfare Reform Efforts.* Washington, DC: General Accounting Office. May 1994. 28 pp. GAO/HEHS-94-112.

Finds that efforts to assist teen mothers could result in more effective welfare reform outcomes.

*Families on Welfare: Sharp Rise in Never-Married Women Reflects Societal Trend.* Washington, DC: General Accounting Office. May 1994. 68 pp. GAO/HEHS-94-92.

Background on those currently receiving support under the AFDC program and the changes in this population in recent years.

*Food Assistance: Potential Impacts of Alternative Systems for Delivering Food Stamp Program Benefits.* Washington, DC: General Accounting Office, 1994. GAO/RCED-95-13.

*Foster Care: Health Needs of Many Young Children are Unknown and Unmet.* Washington, DC: General Accounting Office, May 1995. 35 pp. GAO/HEHS-95-114.

Demonstrates that inadequate information exists about health needs and problems of increasing numbers of children in the foster care system.

*Foster Care: Services to Prevent Out-of-Home Placements Are Limited by Funding Barriers.* Washington, DC: General Accounting Office, June 1993. 30 pp. GAO/HRD-93-76.

Assistance to avert placement in foster care or institutional programs is limited and prevents many family situations from being resolved without such placements.

Hanson, Russell L., and John T. Hartman. *Do Welfare Magnets Attract?* Discussion Paper No. 1028-94. Madison, WI: University of Wisconsin, Institute for Research on Poverty, February 1994.

Addresses the "welfare magnet" theory that higher AFDC benefits attract low income families to migrate.

*HHS/ACF-Welfare Reform: Section 1115 Waiver Authority.* Washington, DC: Department of Health and Human Services, 1995. 150 pp.

One of a series of HHS reports on the status of AFDC Section 1115 waiver projects.

*JOBS and JTPA: Tracking Spending Outcomes and Program Performance.* Washington, DC: General Accounting Office, 1994. 45 pp. GAO/HEHS-94-177.

Looks at ways to examine the results of two of the primary programs for poor people moving into employment.

*Medicaid: Alternatives for Improving Distribution of Funds to States.* Washington, DC: General Accounting Office, 1993. 35 pp. GAO/HRD-93-112FS.

Examines possible alternatives to present system of Medicaid funding in the states.

*Medicaid: States Turn to Managed Care to Improve Access and Control.* Washington, DC: General Accounting Office, 1993. 55 pp. GAO/HRD-93-46.

Looks at the increasing trend to enroll Medicaid recipients in managed care programs as a way to control health care costs.

*Medicaid: Restructuring Approaches Leave Many Questions.* Washington, DC: General Accounting Office, April 1995. 25 pp. GAO/HEHS-95-103.

Provides information on proposals for restructuring Medicaid, comparing different approaches and their implications for federal-state financing.

*Medicaid: States Expand Coverage for Pregnant Women, Infants, and Children.* Washington, DC: General Accounting Office, 1989. 22 pp. GAO/HRD-89-90.

Examines the extent to which states have exercised options to expand coverage for certain needy groups.

*Multiple Employment Training Programs: Conflicting Requirements Underscore Need for Change.* Washington, DC: General Accounting Office, 1994. 50 pp. GAO/T-HEHS-94-120.

Dozens of job related programs exist and have different requirements, creating a lack of coordination and inefficiency. This report looks at the ways in which uniformity could be achieved.

*Multiple Employment Training Programs: Major Overhaul Needed to Reduce Costs, Streamline the Bureaucracy, and Improve Results.* Washington, DC: General Accounting Office, 1995. 50 pp. GAO/T-HEHS-95-53.

The federal government's many job programs exist across several agencies and do not work in concert with each other. This report proposes major changes to achieve better results.

*Multiple Employment Training Programs: Most Federal Agencies Do Not Know If Their Programs Are Working Effectively.* Washington, DC: General Accounting Office, 1994. 35 pp. GAO/HEHS-94-88.

Summarizes the lack of knowledge in federal jobs programs that results from inadequate tracking and reporting of efforts.

*Overview of the AFDC Program, FY 1994.* Washington, DC: Department of Health and Human Services, 1995. 250 pp.

HHS's annual summary of data on the AFDC caseload, applications, and demographics.

*Perspective on Welfare Reform.* Hearing before the Senate Committee on Finance, One hundred fourth Congress, First session, 104-339, Document 96-0145-P.

Robison, Susan. *State Child Welfare Reform: Toward a Family-Based Policy.* Denver: National Conference of State Legislatures. 59 pp.

This volume reports on a study conducted by the National Conference of State Legislatures that attempted to find out the nature of state legislative initiatives designed to develop family-based child welfare public policy.

*Restructuring Public Welfare Administration to Meet the Needs of People in an Urban Society: A Report.* Washington, DC: U.S. Department of Health, Education, and Welfare, 1966. 16 pp.

A report of a conference attended by representatives from 11 states and 12 large cities to study the problems of helping "people in need," now primarily of historical interest.

*Social Security: Federal Disability Programs Face Major Issues.* Washington, DC: General Accounting Office, March 1995. Testimony. 15 pp. GAO/HEHS-95-97.

Disability programs for poor people are also part of the welfare reform debate. Examines some of the issues involved in altering the programs.

*Social Security: New Functional Assessments for Children Raise Eligibility Questions.* Washington, DC: General Accounting Office, 1995. 35 pp. GAO/HEHS-95-66.

Child SSI recipients face their own controversy over eligibility issues and assessments.

*Social Security: Rapid Rise in Children on SSI Disability Rolls Follows New Regulations.* Washington, DC: General Accounting Office, 1994. 35 pp. GAO/HEHS-94-225.

Looks at the increase in children receiving SSI disability benefits.

*Social Security: Major Changes Needed for Disability Benefits for Addicts.* Washington, DC: General Accounting Office, 1994. 45 pp. GAO/HEHS-94-128.

Overview of the issues in the addiction related disability program of SSI.

*Social Security: Disability Rolls Keep Growing, While Explanations Remain Elusive.* Washington, DC: General Accounting Office, 1994. 35 pp. GAO/HEHS-94-34.

Examines the increases in SSI enrollees and the possible sources of recent growth.

Solomon, Carmen, and Jennifer Neisner. *AFDC: Need Standards, Payment Standards, and Maximum Benefits.* Washington, DC: Congressional Research Service Report 95-229 EPW, 1995.

State by state data on AFDC need standards, payment standards, and benefit levels for family sizes of three and four as of July 1, 1994, comparisons of combined AFDC and food stamp benefits to the poverty income guidelines, and a ranking of states by AFDC benefit levels compared to state per capita income.

*Supplemental Security Income: Recipient Population Has Changed as Caseloads Have Burgeoned.* Washington, DC: General Accounting Office, March 1995. Testimony. 17 pp. GAO/HEHS-95-120.

Overview of the changing profile of SSI recipients, including the number of addiction related disability cases.

*Supplemental Security Income: Recipient Population Has Changed as Caseloads Have Burgeoned.* Washington, DC: General Accounting Office, 1995. 30 pp. GAO/HEHS-95-120.

More complete report form of testimony described above.

*Teen Parents and Welfare Reform.* Hearings before the Senate Committee on Finance, One hundred fourth Congress, First Session, 104-349, Document number 96-0152 P.

*Welfare Dependency: Coordinated Community Efforts Can Better Serve Young At-Risk Teen Girls.* Washington, DC: General Accounting Office. May 1995. 36 pp. GAO/HEHS/RCED-95-108.

Provides a description of the health of girls at-risk and a summary of social service providers' views on how their needs are addressed in urban communities.

*Welfare Reform Charts.* Washington, DC: U.S. Department of Labor and U.S. Department of Health, Education, and Welfare, 1971. unpaginated.

Interesting from a historical standpoint, this collection of charts was prepared and published to depict the need for welfare reform and to outline changes proposed by President Richard Nixon.

*Welfare Reform Wrap-up.* Hearing before the Senate Committee on Finance, One hundred fourth Congress, First session, 27 April 1995, 104-327. ISBN 0-160-52273-0.

*Welfare to Work: Current AFDC Program Not Sufficiently Focused on Employment.* Washington, DC: General Accounting Office. December 1994. GAO/HEHS-95-28.

This report offers several criticisms of the JOBS program. One, it serves too few AFDC recipients in general. Two, it serves too few recipients at risk of long stays on AFDC. Three, it is insufficiently focused on recipients' employment as its long-term goal.

*Welfare to Work: JOBS Automated Systems Do Not Focus on Program's Employment Objective.* Washington, DC: General Accounting Office. June 1994. 21 pp. GAO/HEHS-94-44.

Reviews the assistance provided to states in developing information collection about the JOBS program.

*Welfare to Work: JOBS Participation Rate Data Unreliable for Assessing States' Performance.* Washington, DC: General Accounting Office. 1993. GAO/HRD-93-73.

The JOBS program has not produced reliable information about required participation rates, resulting in inadequate facts on which to base an assessment of state performance.

*Welfare to Work: Measuring Outcomes for JOBS Participants.* April 1995. 43 pp. GAO/HEHS-95-86.

Examines the use of outcomes measures by federal and state government to determine whether JOBS program participants are finding employment and leaving the AFDC program.

*Welfare to Work: Most AFDC Training Programs Not Emphasizing Job Placement.* Washington, DC: General Accounting Office. May 1995. 91 pp. GAO/HEHS-95-113.

Information on JOBS programs emphasizing job placement, subsidized employment, or work experience, and factors that hinder efforts to move welfare recipients into jobs.

*Welfare to Work: Participants' Characteristics and Services Provided in JOBS.* Washington, DC: General Accounting Office. May 1995. 29 pp. GAO/HEHS-95-93.

Profiles who is and is not being served under the JOBS program, the range of services being offered, and the implications of meeting need in a time of limited welfare programs.

## Reports (Nongovernmental Agencies)

*AFDC Program Parameters by State, 1988-1995.* Washington, DC: Congressional Research Service, 1995.

Shows AFDC benefits in January 1995 for the 50 states, the District of Columbia, and the territories of Puerto Rico, the Virgin Islands, and Guam. Also shows the change in benefit levels since 1988 and provides a comparison of benefit levels to the HHS poverty guidelines.

*AFDC Program Rules for Advocates: An Overview.* New York: Center on Social Welfare Policy and Law, 1993. Publication #160. 200 pp.

*An Analysis of the Personal Responsibility Act: Summary.* Washington, DC: Center on Budget and Policy Priorities, 1994. 50 pp.

Summarizes the possible effects of the Republicans' Personal Responsibility Act. It notes that the PRA proposes deep cuts in a broad range of programs for low-income households and eliminates the entitlement status for most major low-income benefit programs, including AFDC, SSI, and food stamps.

*Beyond Stereotypes: What State AFDC Studies on Length of Stay Tell Us about Welfare as a "Way of Life."* Washington, DC: Center on Law and Social Policy, 1993. 34 pp.

A review of state studies on the length of time recipients are on AFDC, and the implications of these findings.

Danziger, Sandra, and Sherrie Kossoudji. *When Welfare Ends: Subsistence Strategies of Former GA Recipients: Final Report of the General Assistance Project.* Ann Arbor, MI: University of Michigan School of Social Work, 1995.

Assesses the impact of the elimination of the General Assistance (GA) program in Michigan, two years after the cuts were made.

*Examples of Litigation Issues in the AFDC Program.* New York: Center on Social Welfare Policy and Law, 1990. Publication #163. 25 pp.

*The Family Support Act of 1988: Mountain or Molehill, Retreat or Reform.* New York: Center on Social Welfare Policy and Law, 1989. Publication #10. 25 pp.

*Federal Welfare Reform: A Preliminary Guide for States.* Washington, DC: Children's Defense Fund, 1996. 35pp.

Assesses the key decisions that will accompany implementation of welfare reform. Provides background data on poverty, including housing costs.

*Fiscal Survey of the States.* Washington, DC: National Governors' Association, 1994.

An annual survey of state fiscal data.

*FRAC's Guide to the Food Stamp Program.* Washington, DC: Food Research and Action Center, 1994.

This manual reviews the food stamp program rules and provides citations to the statute, regulations, and relevant court cases.

Greenstein, Robert. *Attempts to Dismiss the Census Poverty Data.* Washington, DC: Center on Budget and Policy Priorities, 1995. 12 pp.

An analysis of Heritage Foundation positions on poverty trends.

Greenstein, Robert, and David Super. *The Child Nutrition Block Grants.* Washington, DC: Center on Budget and Policy Priorities, 1995. 10 pp.

Studies current proposals to block grant programs targeted to child nutrition.

Hartman, Ann. *Out of the Arms of Mothers: What Will Happen to Children if Proposed Family Income Support Cuts Leave Some Parents Unable to Care for Them.* New York: Center on Social Welfare Policy and Law, Publication No. 812, June 1995.

Proposals to deny cash assistance to families after sixty months could force children into foster care just because their families are poor. Institutional care and foster care have both short-term and long-term negative effects on children, are in short supply, and are much more expensive than income support programs like Aid to Families with Dependent Children (AFDC).

Harvey, Stefan. *WIC 20th Anniversary Background Packet.* Washington, DC: Center on Budget and Policy Priorities, 1994.

Includes brief history of the WIC program, research findings, and other information.

Hofferth, Sandra L., and Duncan Chaplin. *Caring for Young Children While Parents Work: Public Policies and Private Strategies.* Washington, DC: The Urban Institute, 1994. 55 pp.

Based on a study of a national sample of mothers who had given birth in the previous year, the report concludes that the level of AFDC payments consistently affects the return to work.

*Holding the Bag: The Effect on State and Local Government of the Emerging Fiscal Agenda in the 104th Congress.* Washington, DC: Center on Budget and Policy Priorities, 1995. 32 pp. Individual fact sheets for each of the 50 states are also available.

Analyzes how benefits and services provided by state and local governments could be affected by proposals moving through Congress.

*Issues in Developing a Formula to Allocate Food Stamp Block Grant Funds Among States.* Washington, DC: Center on Budget and Policy Priorities, 1995. 7 pp.

Looks at the results in the food and nutrition programs of using a block grant approach to funding.

Korenman, Sanders, Jane E. Miller, John E. Sjaastad. *Long-Term Poverty and Child Development in the United States.* University of Wisconsin-Madison: Institute for Research on Poverty.

Finds that developmental deficits caused by childhood poverty are approximately twice as great for children who suffer long term poverty than for those who suffer short time poverty.

Korenman, Sanders, and Jane E. Miller. *Poverty and Children's Nutritional Status in the United States.* University of Wisconsin-Madison: Institute for Research on Poverty, 1994.

Examines the effect of persistent poverty on children's nutritional status. Finds that studies which examine the consequences of poverty by looking at short term factors may significantly understate the consequences of persistent poverty.

Lazere, Edward. *In Short Supply: The Growing Affordable Housing Gap.* Washington, DC: Center on Budget and Policy Priorities, 1995. 45 pp.

Low cost rental housing was in a record short supply in 1993. This analysis of the American Housing Survey shows the problems of poor renters.

*Legislative History of the Family Support Act.* New York: Center on Social Welfare Policy and Law, 1988. Publication #111. 15 pp.

Leonard, Paul, and Edward Lazere. *A Place to Call Home: The Low Income Housing Crisis in 44 Major Metropolitan Areas.* Washington, DC: Center on Budget and Policy Priorities, 1992. 84 pp.

Overview of the housing problems, including affordability, in major urban areas of the country.

Mann, Cindy. *A Medicaid Block Grant is Likely to Lead to an Inequitable Distribution of Federal Funds.* Washington, DC: Center on Budget and Policy Priorities, 1995. 10 pp.

Looks at the consequences of block granting Medicaid funds and finds that this will result in funding not corresponding to need.

Mann, Cindy. *The Impact of Capping Federal Medicaid Payments to the States.* Washington, DC: Center on Budget and Policy Priorities, 1995. 13 pp.

Summarizes the effect of creating a limit on the federal Medicaid payment system and examines the potential consequences of such policy.

Maqri, Michele R., and Jerry Abboud. *State Child Welfare: Statutes and Implementation Patterns.* Denver: National Conference of State Legislatures, 1984. 36 pp.

Thirty-seven states responded to a questionnaire about legislative actions designed to deal with child welfare issues.

May, Richard. *1993 Poverty and Income Trends: A Collection of Times Series Data on Poverty and Income Distribution.* Washington, DC: Center on Budget and Policy Priorities, 1995. 93 pp.

Statistical tables on poverty and income.

National Conference of Catholic Bishops. *Economic Justice for All: Pastoral Letter on Catholic Social Teaching and the U.S. Economy.* Washington, DC: Office of Publishing and Promotion Services, 1986.

Presents the theological basis for social programs to assist the poor.

Nichols, Marion, and Kathryn Porter. *General Assistance Programs: Gaps in the Safety Net.* Washington, DC: Center on Budget and Policy Priorities, 1995. 76 pp.

Nichols, Marion, Jon Dunlap, and Scott Barkin. *National General Assistance Survey, 1992.* Washington, DC: Center on Budget and Policy Priorities and National Conference of State Legislatures, 1992. 45 pp.

*On, Wisconsin?: What's Wrong with the "Work Not Welfare" Waiver.* Washington, DC: Center on Law and Social Policy, 1994. 26 pp.

Analyzes the primary components of Wisconsin's welfare waiver which ends AFDC cash assistance after 2 years.

Rees, Susan, and Maybelle Taylor Bennett. *Block Grants: Missing the Target.* Washington, DC: Coalition on Human Needs (CHN), 1987.

This 1987 CHN study examines the implementation of four federal block grant programs in some states in the 1980s. The block grants covered here are the Chapter 2 Education Block Grant, the Job Training Partnership Act (JTPA), the Small Cities Community Development Block Grant, and the Title XX Social Services Block Grant.

Riccio, James, Daniel Friedlander, and Stephen Freedman. *Gain: Benefits, Costs, and Three-Year Impacts of a Welfare-to-Work*

*Program.* New York: Manpower Development and Research Corporation, 1994.

This final report on California's GAIN program depicts the mandatory program combining job search with basic education and other education and training programs. Subsequently, most families were receiving AFDC benefits, and more were still in poverty.

Roberts, Paula, and Jacqueline Finkel. *Establishing Paternity for Children Receiving AFDC: What's Wrong and What's Right with the Current System.* Washington, DC: Center for Law and Social Policy, October 1994.

A survey of state child support (IV-D) agencies concerning their paternity establishment procedures.

Romero, Carol J. *JTPA Programs and Adult Women on Welfare: Using Training to Raise AFDC Recipients Above Poverty.* Washington, DC: National Commission for Employment Policy, 1994.

This study examines the effectiveness of JTPA programs in placing AFDC recipients into jobs and moving them above the poverty line. The report concludes that while JTPA and similar programs can be effective in moving families out of poverty, more would be needed if two-year time limits on benefits were put into place.

*The Rush to "Reform": 1992 State AFDC Legislative and Waiver Actions.* Washington, DC: Center on Law and Social Policy, 1992. 90 pp.

Key research findings on major issues, and state legislative developments.

Seefeldt, Kristin S., and Pamela A. Holcomb. *Welfare Reform in 1993: State JOBS Programs and Waivers.* Washington, DC: The Urban Institute, 1994.

Summarizes a 1993 telephone survey of state JOBS program administrators on the status of JOBS, implementation trends, state welfare reform developments, and proposals to time limit AFDC.

Shapiro, Isaac, and Scott Barancik. *Where Have All the Dollars Gone? A State-by-State Analysis of Income Disparities Over the*

*1980s.* Washington, DC: Center on Budget and Policy Priorities, 1992. 54 pp.

Shapiro, Isaac. *White Poverty in America.* Washington, DC: Center on Budget and Policy Priorities, 1992. 54 pp.

Although many stereotype America's poor as being from racial and ethnic minorities, poverty among whites predominates in many areas. This report examines its characteristics.

*Should Federal Food Assistance Programs be Converted to Block Grants?* Washington, DC: Center on Budget and Policy Priorities, 1995. 21 pp.

Overview of the issues in a block grant program of food assistance.

*Striking Out: Republicans Offer a Troubling Vision of Welfare Reform.* Washington, DC: Center on Law and Social Policy (CLASP), 1994. 40 pp.

Analyzes key provisions of House Republican welfare reform initiative.

*Survey of State Welfare Reforms.* Washington, DC: National Governors' Association, 1995. 70 pp.

Summarizes welfare reforms implemented or being considered in 48 states.

*Wasting America's Future.* Washington, DC: Children's Defense Fund, 1994. 150 pp. ISBN 0-674-16082-7.

Examines the variety of ways in which increasing and continuing child poverty undermine future health and productivity in the U.S.

*Welfare Cutback Litigation, 1991-1993.* New York: Center on Social Welfare Policy and Law, 1993. Publication #166. 15 pp.

An overview of litigation related to state program cutbacks.

*Wisconsin's Teen Welfare Waiver: An Analysis of the Parental and Family Responsibility Demonstration Project.* Washington, DC: Center on Law and Social Policy, 1992. 17 pp.

Examines the teen provisions of the Wisconsin welfare waiver.

Wolfe, Barbara, and Steven Hill. *The Health, Earnings Capacity, and Poverty of Single-Mother Families.* Institute for Research on Poverty, University of Wisconsin-Madison, 1993.

Some 20 percent of single mothers have substantial health problems and are unlikely to be able to earn enough to escape poverty.

# Periodicals

*Client News.* New York: Center on Social Welfare Policy and Law.

A publication designed for welfare recipient organizations and lay advocates that summarizes recent developments in welfare law. Published three times yearly.

*Index and Summary of Welfare Cases.* New York: Center on Social Welfare Policy and Law. Publication #103. 5pp.

Summarizes and classifies welfare cases. Quarterly editions combined in an annual edition.

*Library Bulletin.* New York: Center on Social Welfare Policy and Law. Publication #100. 5 pp.

A monthly report that describes recent publications, court decisions, waiver activity, and federal agency notices.

*Loyola Poverty Law Review.* New Orleans, LA: Loyola University School of Law. Two issues yearly.

*Reference and Statistical Sources for Legal Research in the AFDC and General Assistance Programs.* New York: Center on Social Welfare Policy and Law. Publication #161. 15 pp.

A compendium of research and reference sources that is published twice yearly.

*Welfare Reform News.* New York: Center on Social Welfare Policy and Law. Publication #105.

A monthly report on new welfare reform developments.

# Nonprint Resources 9

Information about public welfare and welfare reform is available in nonprint form, most commonly on films and videocassettes and through web sites on the Internet. Most of the available films and videocassettes focus primarily on issues of public welfare in general, with relatively little attention paid to issues of reform. These resources are most valuable, therefore, to provide background for issues of reform. This chapter lists examples of film and videocassette resources, audiocassettes, and web site sources.

## Films and Videocassettes

**Children in Need**
*Type:* VHS, $\frac{3}{4}$ U-matic cassette
*Age:* College and adult
*Length:* 60 min.
*Cost:* $125
*Date:* 1989
*Source:* PBS Video
1320 Braddock Pl.
Alexandria, VA 22314
(703) 739-5380
(703) 739-5269 (fax)
(800) 344-3337

A description of programs through which businesses, community groups, government agencies, and teachers work to improve the lot of children in the United States.

**Down and Out in America**
*Type:* VHS, Beta
*Age:* Junior high school to adult
*Length:* 60 min.
*Cost:* $29.95
*Date:* 1986
*Source:* MPI Home Video
15825 Rob Roy Dr.
Oak Forest, IL 60452
(708) 687-7881
(708) 687-3797 (fax)

A well-known film about homelessness in both urban and rural America.

**Faces of Poverty**
*Type:* VHS
*Age:* Junior high school and adult
*Length:* 20 min.
*Cost:* $29.95
*Date:* 1987
*Source:* EcuFilm
810 Twelfth Ave., S.
Nashville, TN 37203
(615) 242-6277
(800) 251-4091

Attempts to deal with "conventional wisdom" about the poor, such as the belief that the unemployed could find work if they wanted to and that poor people are satisfied to survive on welfare.

**Poverty: Closing the Gap**
*Type:* $3/4$ U-matic cassette and, by special order,
other formats
*Age:* High school and adult
*Length:* varies according to format
*Cost:* varies according to format
*Date:* 1976
*Source:* The Cinema Guild

1697 Broadway, Suite 506
New York, NY 10019
(212) 246-5522
(212) 246-5525 (fax)
(800) 723-5522

Describes the experiences of a business executive who gave up his job to work with poor people, helping them to receive the benefits for which they are legally qualified. An interview with John Sewell, of the National Welfare Rights League, is included.

### Poverty in America

*Type:* ³/₄ U-matic cassette
*Age:* High school and adult
*Length:* 28 min.
*Cost:* n/a
*Date:* 1980
*Source:* Dallas County Community College District
Center for Educational Telecommunications
Dallas Telecourses
9596 Walnut St.
Dallas, TX 75243
(214) 952-0330
(214) 952-0329 (fax)

A historical review of the problem of poverty in America from the Depression to the present day.

### Poverty Shock: Any Woman's Story

*Type:* VHS, Beta, ³/₄ U-matic cassette
*Age:* High school and adult
*Length:* 29 min.
*Cost:* Call for information
*Date:* 1989
*Source:* Centre Communications
1800 30th St., Suite 207
Boulder, CO 80301
(303) 444-1166
(303) 444-1168 (fax)
(800) 886-1166

An investigation of the "feminization of poverty," a condition that has become increasingly common in the United States in recent decades.

**The Southern Poverty Law Center**
*Type:* VHS
*Age:* College to adult
*Length:* 18 min.
*Cost:* Call for information
*Date:* 1990
*Source:* University of Washington
Educational Media Collection
Kane Hall, DG-10
Seattle, WA 98195
(206) 543-9909
(206) 685-7892 (fax)

A documentary about the organization founded in 1971 by lawyer Morris Dees to aid the poor and defend their civil rights.

**Welfare**
*Age:* High school and adult
*Length:* 167 min.
*Cost:* $350
*Date:* 1982
*Source:* Zipporah Vilms, Inc.
1 Richdale Ave.
Cambridge, MA 02140
(617) 576-3603
(617) 864-8006 (fax)

A detailed analysis of the issues involved in the current welfare system, including divorce, unemployment, abandonment and abuse of children, problems of old age, health problems, and housing.

**Who Lives, Who Dies?**
*Type:* VHS, $^3/_4$ U-matic cassette
*Age:* High school and adult
*Length:* 55 min.
*Cost:* Call for information
*Date:* 1988
*Source:* Filmakers Library, Inc.
124 E. 40th
New York, NY 10016
(212) 808-4980
(212) 808-4983 (fax)

A portrayal of the increasingly common practice of limiting health care on the basis of income as hospitals and clinics decline to provide services for the poor.

**Women: The New Poor**

*Type:* VHS
*Age:* Adult
*Length:* 28 min.
*Cost:* $250
*Date:* 1990
*Source:* Women Make Movies
462 Broadway, Suite 501
New York, NY 10013
(212) 925-0606
(212) 925-2052 (fax)

Interviews with four single and divorced women illuminate an increasingly serious problem in American society, the difficulty of making a living and providing adequate care for their children in modern society.

# Audio Resources

The Center for Law and Social Policy (CLASP) is one of the leading policy organizations involved in the welfare reform debate. During 1995–1996, CLASP initiated a series of national conference calls with participants around the country. These calls involved a small number of panelists offering insight on various aspects of the debate. Participants were permitted to email or FAX questions to the panelists during the call. The calls were audio taped for distribution to a wider audience. The audio tapes are available for $10 each from CLASP: 1616 P Street NW, Suite 150; Washington, D.C. 20036; (202) 328-5140, or fax: (202) 328-5195.

# Federal Web Sites

## Bureau of Labor Statistics

http://stats.bis.gov/
LABSTAT database with labor figures, documents, and tables

## Census Bureau

http://www.census.gov/
Facts and figures on the U.S. population, including data access tools, maps, and a BBS

## Department of Education (USEd)

http://www.ed.gov/
Includes education guides, statistics, and connection to agency server

## Department of Health and Human Services (HHS)

http://www.os.dhhs.gov/
A guide to grants, data, research and a topic index

## Department of Housing and Urban Development (HUD)

http://www.hud.gov/
Policy and program information

## Department of Labor (DOL)

http://lcweb.loc.gov/global/executive/labor.html
Bureau of Labor Statistics, OSHA, and Library of Congress connection

## FedWorld

http://www.fedworld.gov/
Links to over 100 federal bulletin board systems

## Government Page

http://www.ucsb.edu/uc/government.html
A starting point for information about state and federal government

## Government Printing Office

http://www.access.gpo.gov/
Congressional pictorial database, texts of Federal Register, bills, and other federal documents

# Political Parties

## Democratic Party Committee

email: info@dpc.senate.gov
World Wide Web site: ftp://ftp.senate.gov/committee/Dem-Policy/general/dpc.html

## Republican Party

World Wide Web site: www.rnc.org

## U.S. House of Representatives

http://www.house.gov/
Schedules for legislative activity, phone numbers of members, and current House action

### Other House Web Sites
House Gopher:  gopher://gopher:house.gov:70/1
House Web Site:  http://www.house.gov/
House Democratic Caucus:
http://www.house.gov/demcaucus/welcome.html
House Democratic Leadership:
http://www.house.gov/democrats/
House Republican Conference:
http://www.house.gov/gop/HRCHome.html

### House Committees
slabmgnt@hr.house.gov
Economic and educational opportunities, subcommittee on employer-employee relations

resource@hr.house.gov
Resources

## Congressional Black Caucus

http://drum.ncsc.org/~carter/CBC.html

## U.S. Senate

**Senate Gopher:** gopher://ftp.senate.gov:70/
**Senate Democratic Policy Committee:**
ftp://www.senate.gov/committee/Dem-Policy/general/dpc.html
**Senate Republican Policy Committee:**
ftp://www.senate.gov/committee/repub-policy/general/rpc.html
**Senate Committee on Aging:** mailbox@aging.senate.gov

The most current information about the Senate is available on the University of Michigan Library Gopher. Gopher to the University of Michigan Library Gopher or telnet to una.hh.lib.umich.edu Login as gopher. Path: Social Sciences/Government/U.S. Government: Legislative Branch/E-Mail Addresses.

## Other Congressional Sites

**Legislative Web Site:**
http://govtdoc.law.csuohio.edu/legpage.html
House and Senate services, including links to the House Home Page and the Senate gopher.
**Thomas Legislative Information on the Internet:**
http:// thomas.loc.gov
Full text versions of all bills from the 103d and 104th Congresses, the *Congressional Record,* and other House of Representatives information.

# White House Internet Addresses

The White House has Internet e-mail IDs. To write the President fill in the To: prompt of a regular e-mail memo form with this address: president@whitehouse.gov
To write to the Vice President use: vice.president@whitehouse. gov

# Glossary

**ADC** Aid to Dependent Children, the predecessor of AFDC; created by the Social Security Act of 1935.

**AFDC** Aid to Families with Dependent Children, the primary contemporary cash assistance program for poor people.

**AFDC-UP** Aid to Families with Dependent Children—Unemployed Parent program.

**appropriations** The amount of funding Congress provides for a program or line item in a given year. Language sometimes sets the terms under which funds may be spent.

**authorization** Legislation that establishes or continues a federal program or agency, specifies its general goals and conduct, and usually sets a ceiling on the amount of money that can be appropriated for it.

**block grants** Funding allocations to states that can be used for a variety of purposes. Block grants are funded by annual appropriations by Congress and allocated to states by formula. Block grants usually provide considerable flexibility to governors for delivering the services outlined in the block grant. Block grants in the welfare reform debate have been portrayed as a positive step by Republican legislators, who emphasize their potential for innovation, autonomy, and flexibility without federal restrictions on how or where funds are spent.

**budget authority** Authority to enter into obligations that will result in immediate or future outlays involving federal funds. Appropriation bills provide budget authority.

**Budget Enforcement Act** Passed in 1990, this act established caps on discretionary spending in each area of federal spending—defense, domestic, and international. It also prohibited transfers between these categories. These "walls" between spending categories expired after Fiscal Year 1993. Now there is one cap for all discretionary spending.

**capped entitlement** An entitlement on which an overall annual funding limit is placed and funding is distributed by formula.

**categorical grant** An allocation of funds for a particular programmatic purpose.

**child exclusion** Provision in state AFDC programs to prevent an increase in benefits when an additional child is born to a mother already receiving benefits.

**Child Support Enforcement (CSE)** A federal program providing matching funds to states to assist in enforcing the support obligations of absent parents, to locate absent parents, and to establish paternity and support orders. States must provide child support enforcement services to persons receiving AFDC, Medicaid, and some foster care benefits.

**Child Support Enforcement and Assurance (CSEA)** A system to guarantee some child support to custodial parents, even if the absent parent fails to pay child support.

**Community Work Experience (CWEP)** A portion of the JOBS program that states can make available to participants. CWEP provides training and experience for individuals who cannot otherwise obtain employment.

**concurrent budget resolution** A budget resolution passed by both houses of Congress, but not requiring the signature of the president. The annual budget resolution presents both fiscal aggregates such as total budget authority, outlays and deficit, and a subdivision of spending by functional category for the year. May also include binding instructions on the level of savings each committee must produce. (See **reconciliation.**)

**continuing resolution** Legislation that extends appropriations for specific ongoing programs when the regular appropriation has not been enacted by the beginning of the fiscal year (1 October).

**debt ceiling** A statutory limit imposed on the total outstanding federal debt. The ceiling can be raised or lowered through an act of Congress.

**discretionary programs** Programs funded by annual congressional appropriations bills, except for "appropriated entitlements" such as Medicaid or veterans' compensation. Under the Budget Enforcement Act, these expenditures are capped.

**discretionary spending cap** Limits placed on the total amount of budget authority and outlays for discretionary programs that Congress can provide in a given fiscal year.

**EITC** The Earned Income Tax Credit, a tax credit available to working poor people. The EITC is intended to provide tax relief from the Social Security payroll tax and to increase work incentives.

**Electronic Benefits Transfer (EBT)** Use of cards similar to bank debit cards to allow beneficiaries of welfare programs to access their benefits electronically, rather than through the use of mailed paper checks and cash.

**entitlement** Program mandating the payment of benefits to any person meeting eligibility requirements established by statute. The amount spent is not controlled by annual congressional appropriations. Entitlement programs include Social Security, Medicare, AFDC, and Medicaid.

**ESL** English as a Second Language

**family cap** A ceiling on the dollar amount of benefits a family will receive.

**family preservation** Programs aimed at keeping families together and working intensively on their problems without removing children from the home.

**family unification** Efforts to return children to the home through the provision of adequate housing or other measures.

**FSA** The Family Support Act of 1988, the previous comprehensive welfare reform effort that created the JOBS program.

**fiscal year (FY)** The federal government's accounting period, which begins on 1 October and ends on 30 September.

**food stamps** A national program to improve the ability of poor families to purchase food by providing monthly coupons for a specific dollar amount. The coupons can be used in most grocery stores.

**formula fight** Federal funding arrangements set in law are known as formulas. Inevitably, the choices between competing priorities and formula details pit one state's interests and potential funding totals against others. The formulas dictate the division of billions of dollars.

**formula funding** Federal funding arrangements are set in law and known as formulas. In the AFDC program, for example, while each state determines what dollar amount of benefits to pay to a family, the federal government pays its share of that figure based on a formula tied to per capita income. The federal government pays between 50 and 70 percent of the cost of benefits, depending on the state. The formula combines with the entitlement status of AFDC to provide benefits for as many persons as qualify in a given state. This approach also means that when a recession occurs the flow of federal dollars will increase.

**GED** General Educational Development certificate, a program that represents a general educational attainment level for those who do not complete high school.

**General Assistance** State- and county-funded programs designed to provide basic benefits to low-income people who are not eligible for federally funded cash assistance. Jurisdictions determine general assistance benefit levels, eligibility criteria, and length of eligibility.

**JOBS** The Job Opportunities and Basic Skills Training Program, created by the Family Support Act of 1988. The JOBS is a program focused on work, education, and training opportunities for AFDC recipients.

**JTPA** The Job Training Partnership Act, a Department of Labor block grant program to states for training or retraining eligible persons in unsubsidized employment in the private sector.

**lump sum** A method of payment to states or other jurisdictions that permits the recipients jurisdiction to make determinations about the allocation of funds.

**maintenance of effort** The concept that, under changed legal requirements, a state or other government must continue to spend the same amount of money for the use in question. For example, a maintenance of effort requirement in creating block grants to the states for cash assistance for poor families would require that a state continue spending the same amount of money, even if the new law allows the state to change eligibility requirements, impose time limits, or require other actions by recipients. Maintenance of effort would require a state to continue contributing the same amount of funding and not shift its spending functions.

**noncompliance** Failure to meet some program requirement, such as attendance in education programs, or to maintain sobriety.

**Pay-As-You-Go (or Pay-Go)** A provision of the Budget Enforcement Act of 1990. Requires that any entitlement or tax proposal include provisions for financing. New entitlement or tax proposals must be paid for by raising new revenue or cutting existing entitlement programs. Thus, changes in entitlement programs or revenues must be deficit neutral.

**payment standard** In the AFDC program, a figure that is 100 percent or less of the standard of need. Benefits are calculated by subtracting certain forms of income from the state standard of need.

**PIC** The Private Industry Council, the local agency that administers federal employment and training funds, such as the JTPA.

**rainy day fund** A fund of federal dollars that would provide additional assistance in an economic downturn or if a state experiences an unforeseen difficulty that makes block grant funds inadequate to meet need.

**reconciliation** The process used by Congress to amend tax and entitlement programs to meet the instructions in the budget resolution.

**rescission** A statutory midyear reduction or cancellation in previously appropriated funds.

**safety net** The array of benefits and assistance available to meet basic needs, such as food, housing, income, and health care.

**sanctions** Penalties attached to a recipient's failure to meet a specific program requirement, such as appearing for a scheduled appointment. This might result in a sanction, such as being dropped from the welfare rolls for a period of time.

**scoring** A budget function under federal law that requires that changes proposed in the federal budget be "scored" for their overall budget effect. In the welfare reform debate, the official scoring agency, the Congressional Budget Office, estimated that it would cost about $10 billion to provide child care and job training for families that would be required to work under the welfare program changes. Controversy arises in the scoring process when different economic assumptions are used, such as whether the economy will grow and at what rate.

**sequestration** The withholding or cancellation of funds pursuant to the Gramm-Rudman-Hollings Act, the 1985 deficit-reduction law. Sequestered funds are permanently canceled.

**standard of need** In the AFDC program, the state establishes an income figure it determines is needed for basic consumption items to be covered. The standard of need is criticized as being too low to cover high housing costs in some areas, for example.

**Supplemental Security Income (SSI)** A means-tested, federally administered income assistance program authorized by Title XVI of the Social Security Act. The SSI was begun in 1974 to provide monthly cash payments in accordance with uniform, nationwide standards of eligibility for the needy aged, blind, and disabled. Disabled persons are those unable to engage in any substantial gainful activity by reason of a serious impairment that will result in death or that has lasted or will last for a continuous period of at least 12 months. Some states provide a state SSI supplement.

**time limits** In welfare programs, the length of time a recipient will be eligible for benefits without an additional requirement. For example, a recipient might be required to become employed after receiving benefits for two years.

**welfare reform** Welfare is typically identified with the AFDC program, the best-known source of income support for poor children. Welfare reform typically means any significant change to the scope, design, or administration of AFDC. In the current public debate, however, all forms of support for poor people, including housing, food, health care, and more, have been labeled as welfare.

**WIC** Women, Infants, and Children nutrition program.

**working poor** Working poor people are not the focus of current welfare reform efforts, although they are often just a step away from assistance. These are low-wage workers who do not receive direct government support but face economic problems related to cost of child care, lack of buying power, and need for health insurance.

**work requirements** Rules attached to receipt of benefits, such as the expectation that a welfare recipient will find employment and move off the welfare rolls within a stated period, such as two years.

# Index

Mary Ellen Hombs has long been an advocate for poor people. From 1971 to 1988 she lived and worked with homeless people in Washington, D.C.'s Community for Creative Non-Violence, helping create and operate emergency, medical, and housing services, as well as being involved in national and local policy advocacy. She has worked with the National Coalition for the Homeless and the Legal Services Homelessness Task Force. She presently works in Boston. She is also the author of *American Homelessness* and *Aids Crisis in America*.